Thrive, don't simply Survive

Thrive, don't simply *Survive*

Passionately Live
the Life You Didn't Plan

KAROL LADD

HOWARD BOOKS
A DIVISION OF SIMON & SCHUSTER
New York London Toronto Sydney

Our purpose at Howard Books is to:
- *Increase faith* in the hearts of growing Christians
- *Inspire holiness* in the lives of believers
- *Instill hope* in the hearts of struggling people everywhere

Because He's coming again!

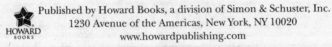 Published by Howard Books, a division of Simon & Schuster, Inc.
1230 Avenue of the Americas, New York, NY 10020
www.howardpublishing.com

Thrive, Don't Simply Survive © 2009 by Karol Ladd

Published in association with The Steve Laube Agency, LLC.

Library of Congress Cataloging-in-Publication Data

Ladd, Karol.
Thrive, don't simply survive : passionately live the life you didn't plan / Karol Ladd.
p. cm.
1. Christian women—Religious life. 2. Consolation. 3. Success—Religious aspects—Christianity. 4. Self-actualization (Psychology)—Religious aspects—Christianity. I. Title.
BV4527.L253 2008
248.8'43—dc22
2008032147

ISBN-13: 978-1-4165-8049-2
ISBN-10:   1-4165-8049-2

1   3   5   7   9   10   8   6   4   2

Edited by Jennifer Stair
Interior design by Davina Mock-Maniscalco

All Scripture quotations, unless otherwise noted, are taken from the *Holy Bible, New Living Translation*. © 1996, 2004. Used by permission of Tyndale House Publishers, Inc., Wheaton, Illinois 60189. All rights reserved. Scriptures marked NIV are taken from the *Holy Bible, New International Version*®. Copyright © 1973, 1978, 1984 by International Bible Society. Scriptures marked MSG are taken from *The Message* by Eugene H. Peterson. © 1993, 1994, 1995, 1996, 2000, 2001, 2002. Used by permission of NavPress Publishing Group. All rights reserved. Scriptures marked CEV are taken from the *Holy Bible, Contemporary English Version*. © 1991, 1995 by the American Bible Society. Used by permission. Scriptures marked ESV are taken from the *English Standard Version*. © 2001 by Crossway Bibles, a division of Good New Publishers. Scriptures marked NKJV are taken from the *New King James Version*. © 1979, 1980, 1982 by Thomas Nelson, Inc. Used by permission. All rights reserved.

Italics in Scripture quotations indicate the author's added emphasis.

Thank you to the women who gave permission to share their stories in this book. Their courage and determination to live joyfully in spite of the difficult surprises that came their way inspires us all. In some cases, names and identifying details have been changed to protect the privacy of the individuals involved.

Contents

Acknowledgments

THANK YOU to all the wonderful women who shared their personal stories to bless the readers of this book. I am especially grateful to Amy, Leslie, and Tammy for their contributions, thoughts, and friendship.

A special thanks to Philis Boultinghouse, Jennifer Stair, and all my friends at Howard Books who devoted their time, hard work, and wise insight to make this book thrive!

None of us knows what the next change is going to be,
what unexpected opportunity is just around the corner,
waiting a few months or a few years to change all the tenor of our lives.

Kathleen Norris

Introduction

This Is Not What I Signed Up For!

Living in an Unpredictable World

We can make our plans, but the LORD determines our steps.

Proverbs 16:9

W HEN DID YOU GROW UP? What I'm really asking is, when did you first begin to realize that life doesn't always turn out fair and happy? Some people grow up early in their lives as a result of difficult childhood experiences, while others take awhile to grow up through life's ups and downs. Some adults still haven't grown up! Honestly, when it really comes down to it, the big question in life is not, will disappointments happen? The broader, more realistic question is, when disappointments happen, how will we deal with them?

This book answers that broader question. When challenges come my way—and trust me, I've had my fair share of challenges—I don't want to simply survive and dog-paddle my way through life. I want to thrive! I have a feeling you do too. *Surviving* implies that we barely make it through the difficulties in life, holding on by our fingernails in order to preserve any sort of normalcy. But *thriving* goes beyond simple survival. It means we rise above disappointing circumstances and experience a joyful and vibrant life despite the challenges. Now I know there are times when all we can do is simply survive, but eventually each of us can come to a place in our lives where we thrive despite the circumstances. Thriving isn't always easy, but it is worth the challenge. Are you willing to leave the discouragement behind? Are you open to seeing what God has around the corner, even if it isn't what you dreamed for your life? Then read on!

Challenges and disappointments come in all shapes and sizes. An unexpected diagnosis, an unwanted divorce, a surprise pregnancy, a broken relationship, a terminated job, a painful car accident, a financial loss, an untimely death, or a wayward child can catch us off guard and turn our lives upside down. Perhaps your life did not turn out as you thought it would, or maybe *you* didn't turn out to be the person you thought you would be, or maybe God didn't do what you expected him to do in your life. Although your dreams have changed, the important thing to remember is you still have a life to live and there are myriad opportunities ahead of you.

When expectations in life change and dreams are dashed, there is potential for a new and different picture to emerge. Certainly we must grieve the loss of our dreams, but then we must decide whether to adapt with grace and anticipation for what God can do, or kick and scream and snarl and blame others. Now, I'm thinking it is pretty obvious which one of these choices creates a thriving woman who passionately lives the life she didn't plan. I'm guessing you would like to be that kind of woman, not a bitter, angry, stuck-in-her-circumstances type of woman. The good news is you can learn to thrive!

> *When expectations in life change and dreams are dashed, there is potential for a new and different picture to emerge.*

Beyond Survival

Though it might seem impossible to you now, you *can* move beyond survival and live passionately and victoriously in your new circumstances. God is a redeeming God who is able to bring freshness to places that seem rotten and decayed. Most important, God is a loving God who will never leave you, even when you feel like you are in the deepest, darkest hole.

How do you embrace the unexpected? How do you joyfully accept the hand you have been dealt and passionately live the life you didn't plan? I wish I could tell you that there is an easy three-step solution to follow, and everything will be grand. Although we would love for life to be that easy, the reality is that life is complicated and there are no easy solutions to life's difficulties. Yet you (yes, you) can learn to thrive in the life you didn't plan. The answer isn't found in three easy steps; rather, it is found in the transforming work of God in our lives. In the pages of this book, you will find encouragement, strength, wisdom, and hope based on the principles of God's Word. My desire is to point you to the only source of true and lasting joy, God himself.

The Bible provides life-changing principles to help us grow and learn as we walk down the winding path of the unexpected. God gives us his Holy Spirit to lead us and guide us in fresh and hope-filled directions. He heals our wounds and gives us strength to move forward. The psalmist reminds us that God redeems our life from the pit and crowns us with love and compassion. He satisfies our desires with good things, so our youth is renewed like the eagle's.[1] *Redeem* doesn't mean God is going to wipe away every difficulty in our lives. Rather, when God redeems a situation He brings something good out of the seemingly dismal circumstances.

God has a plan beyond our broken dreams and dashed expectations. Plan A didn't work out, but God is not finished with the stories of our lives. In this book you will read true stories of women—and a few men too—who have faced a variety of disappointments in their plan As of life and yet have seen God's strength and renewal in plan Bs. We will also glean solid biblical principles on dealing with disappointments, refocusing on new possibilities, and becoming courageous and confident women.

Each chapter begins with powerful quotes from faith-filled men and women and is filled with amazing stories and practical plans to help you face disappointment. I don't want this to be just another book you read and then put on a shelf; my hope is that these chapters will impact your way of living and thinking. That's why I put the Stepping Forward section at the end of each chapter. In this special recap section, I have included Points (a reminder of the key points you learned in the chapter), Passage (a Scripture reading on which you can reflect), Prayer (an opportunity for you to connect with God), and Plan (a practical application to help you live out what you've learned). My prayer is that this book will be a powerful inspiration to you as you face the unpredictability of life one step at a time.

The Choice Is Yours

You may feel as though you have no control over your life, but you actually do have choices! Will you choose to trust a sovereign God who loves you and has a plan for your life, or will you wallow in hopelessness and despair? Will you choose to have a can-do attitude, or will you choose to whine and complain? Will you choose to step up and move forward, or will you choose to stay in a rut? Isn't it great to have choices? You face these same choices every day whether you encounter simple daily disappointments or experience major life letdowns.

Although I can't make those choices for you, I can offer you tools to equip you and inspire you to make positive choices. In a sense, this book is a handbook to help turn discouragement into possibilities, while listening to the voice of our Good Shepherd, who compassionately leads us and guides us along the path. Sometimes that path is a rocky road, but our loving Shepherd will not leave us. He is there to carry us through the difficult crevasses and over the mountaintops to green valleys ahead.

So let's continue our journey down unpredictable roads together. I'm here to encourage you, inspire you, and give you a friendly nudge to stop dwelling on the negatives and instead turn your focus upward and move in a positive new direction. This is your reference guide for the path ahead, providing you with biblical wisdom, encouraging stories, and powerful principles to embrace the unexpected. May your plan-B life radiate the beauty God can bring to you and to those around you.

PART ONE

When Dreams Disappoint

Let nothing disturb thee,
Let nothing affright thee,
All things are passing,
God changeth never.

Saint Teresa of Ávila

Don't let your hearts be troubled.
Trust in God, and trust also in me.

Jesus (John 14:1)

*There is no pit so deep
that God's love is not deeper still.*

Corrie ten Boom

1

Seven Common Disappointments in a Woman's Life

Identifying Your Struggles and Realizing You Are Not Alone

No test or temptation that comes your way is beyond the course of what others have had to face. All you need to remember is that God will never let you down; he'll never let you be pushed past your limit; he'll always be there to help you come through it.

1 Corinthians 10:13 MSG

YOU ARE NOT ALONE. Somehow that statement brings comfort, doesn't it? Knowing someone else is journeying with you offers encouragement and hope. Right now you may be thinking, *I feel so all alone. No one understands my frustration and pain.* Certainly there is no other person who knows exactly how you feel or has experienced the specific grief of your personal disappointment—yet, my friend, I want you to know *you are not alone.*

You are not alone, because there beside you, although you may not see him or feel him, is the God who cares for you. He is the God who sees all, and he invites you to cast your cares on him.[1] Throughout the ages, God has been lovingly reassuring his people,

3

"Do not be afraid, for I am with you."[2] In Psalms, we read David's affirmation of God's presence: "I can never escape from your Spirit! I can never get away from your presence!"[3] Try as we might, we can't hide from God. His loving arms extend wherever we go. God will meet us where we are, with arms open wide, saying, "Come to me, all of you who are weary and carry heavy burdens, and I will give you rest."[4]

I cannot tell you why you are in the seat of disappointment, nor can I answer the question, "Why did God allow this?" The answers aren't always easy or evident. Although we may not understand why God allows the not-so-happy scenarios in our lives, we can still trust his love and care for us. He is a merciful and patient God. You may have been ignoring him for many years, but, my friend, it is never too late to cry out to him. The Bible assures us that if we seek him, we will find him.[5] The God of all comfort loves you and desires a relationship with you.

The Bible describes God as "compassionate and gracious, . . . slow to anger, abounding in love."[6] Isn't that an inviting description? What a wonderful heavenly Father we have! As his children, we can be assured he is with us in the joyful times of our lives as well as in the difficult ones.

Picture with me just for a moment a loving parent who takes her child to the park and the zoo and the ice cream shop. Can you imagine the same parent dropping off her injured child at the hospital and saying, "I know you're in a lot of pain, but I'm busy right now. I'll come back and pick you up later when everything is okay." No, a good parent will lovingly hold her child through the difficult and painful experiences. Now, if a human parent cares for a child in this manner, how much more does our perfect heavenly Father hold us with his gentle loving embrace through the trials we face? Our gracious God will never leave us.

Comforting Bonds

Although your pain is personal, you are not the only one who has experienced pain. We share a common bond with women throughout the ages who have experienced disappointments and loss, both great and small. From Eve in the Garden of Eden all the way to you and me, no one is exempt from experiencing failed dreams and dashed expectations. Not only do we find camaraderie in the common experience

> *Although your pain is personal, you are not the only one who has experienced pain.*

of disillusionment, but we can also find hope from the strength, peace, and blessing other women have experienced through their struggles. Within each story of disenchantment is a nugget of possibility. Of course, no one's story is exactly like yours or mine; however, there still exists in every woman's story an element of hope that can inspire and encourage us.

Personally, I gain strength from knowing other women faced similar disappointments and not only survived, but thrived. If you are like me, you are inspired by the stories of women who passionately lived the lives they didn't plan. Whether we are reading about women in history or present-day accounts, we are heartened to know that we are not the only ones who have faced insurmountable odds or a change in our life direction. Consider my friend Jan's story.

Jan always pictured herself as the mother of girls. In fact, she still has her childhood Barbie collection, which she had planned to someday pass down to her daughters. But Jan wouldn't trade her four sons for the world. She says the one word that describes her life is *adaptation*. Of course, adapting to four sons instead of having daughters has been a relatively easy adaptation to God's plan, compared to adapting to the fact that one of her sons is severely disabled.

When Connor, her third son, was born, Jan and her mother, Dede, recognized that something wasn't quite right. Although the hospital sent him home saying he was healthy, they noticed a few red flags. He didn't cry, and although that may seem nice, Jan and Dede knew it wasn't a good sign. Every feeding was a struggle, and Connor's eyes didn't track movement. Jan and her husband, Patrick, took Connor to doctor after doctor trying to find answers.

As Connor grew, he couldn't walk or talk or feed himself. His full list of disorders includes cerebral palsy, seizure disorder, cortical visual impairment (brain blindness), microcephaly (small head), severe developmental delay, mental retardation, difficulty swallowing, low muscle tone, and immobility. Even now at twelve years old, Connor functions like a newborn, totally dependent on others. He cannot sit up, roll over, feed himself, or talk.

When Connor was two years old, the Wrights' fourth son was born. With a special-needs child and a newborn who both needed full-time care, in addition to their other two sons, Jan soon became physically and emotionally overwhelmed. Each day she seemed to simply survive, trying to get the two older boys off to school and then care for the younger ones with little or no sleep. Jan had wonderful family and friends who helped, but she still felt like she was in the pit of despair with no answers and no hope.

Jan remembers one day when she looked at herself in the mirror, saw her haggard face, and thought, *Who is that woman?* Then in the quietness of the moment, she heard God's voice saying to her, *Are you going to let this kill you, or are you going to rise to the occasion and get on with your life? You have a husband who loves you, and your kids need a functional mommy. You have a lot to keep you going!* She realized that her self-pity, anger, and grief were getting her nowhere.

Jan knew then that it was a moment of decision. Although she didn't have all the answers, it was time to accept her situation and do the best she could for Connor and the rest of her family. She began to open her eyes to God's provision and take positive steps forward. Jan recalls that she and Patrick decided they were not just going to survive this, but chose to thrive in it. (In fact, Jan's words became the inspiration for the title of this book.) They knew they were called to be more than conquerors through Christ.

Jan is honest about her emotional journey through her challenges. She says, "I definitely did not feel adequate. I still don't. But here I am!" By relying on God's strength day by day, she has learned to passionately live the life she didn't plan.

They have endured hardships, but Jan and Patrick wouldn't trade them for all the blessings they have received from having Connor in their family. The Wright family is fun-loving and joyful. They continually reach out to help other people, and their home is always filled with friends. The family bond is strong, and their trust in the Lord has grown deep.

Connor will never walk or talk this side of heaven, but his life is a blessing. He has brought joy to each member of his family. Their journey has been long and challenging, but they are thankful for the life lessons Connor has taught them. Jan readily admits, "I have always felt very ordinary. But I know the Bible is full of ordinary people God called and equipped to do something special."

Jan didn't sign up for the challenges she has faced, yet she has learned to lean on God through her journey. Day by day, God gives Jan what she needs to step up and passionately live the life she didn't plan.

Jan learned not only to adapt, but to live victoriously through her unexpected life challenges. In this chapter, we will explore seven common disappointments women typically face in life. Now I'm not saying that every woman has experienced all seven of these disappointments. Goodness, how depressing would that be? But these seven are the most common ones women experience in life. Most likely you will be nodding your head as you read, saying, "Yes, I can relate to that one and to that one, and boy am I glad I haven't gone through that one!" My purpose here is not to open up your eyes to how miserable you really are, but to help you identify your struggles and recognize you are not alone.

So let's jump in and identify the big seven. Keep in mind, we are not going to deal with how to overcome the disappointments in this chapter (that's what the rest of the book is about); we are simply identifying them.

1. Disappointment with Marriage

Whether you are single, married, or single again, you have probably discovered "living happily ever after" occurs in our favorite fairy tales but not in reality. If you have been married at least a year, you possibly have learned that your husband may not quite live up to the "knight in shining armor" you thought he would be. If you are not married, you may be longing for that special man to come into your life.

Disappointments in marriage include issues regarding finances, personal frustrations, indiscretions, and incompatibility. Maybe the good-looking guy you married in college turned out to be a lazy bum or a flagrant spender who ran you into serious debt. Or your Mr. Faithful turned out to be Mr. Flirt. Or your attentive boyfriend turned out to have the sensitivity of a barn door once you were married.

People surprise us. Sometimes they change, and sometimes they are just plain different than who we thought they were when we married them. Let's face it, marriage is not as easy as we thought it would be. But through the disappointments in marriage, we can still see God's hand at work as he strengthens our ability to love and be loved. Ultimately, we want to continually enrich our marriages, so they can be the best that they can be beyond the disappointments.

Perhaps you are single, though you had hoped and planned to be married by now. Or maybe you planned to live the rest of your life with your husband, only to have weathered divorce or widowhood. Possibly you never thought of yourself as being a single parent, but there you are. Please don't get me wrong—being single is not a negative; it just may not be the place you had planned to be right now. Whether single or married, we can *choose to thrive* no matter what the circumstances.

2. Disappointment with Kids

When it comes to kids, many parents experience frustration, surprise, or concern. Possibly you have a child who doesn't fit into the delightful box society calls the "perfect child." A disability or disease or defiant attitude may have changed the picture of what you always thought your family would look like. Whether it is a young, uncontrollable screamer or a teen running around with the wrong crowd, our kids, more than likely, are not going to be exactly what we envisioned.

When they are grown, our children may not marry who we thought they should, or they may not go into the type of profession we thought they would. You may feel the pain of their poor or sinful choices even when you taught them so carefully to do what is right. They may struggle with addictions. They may have distanced themselves from you or from your faith, and you never thought they would be so far away. Take comfort in the fact that God has a plan for your child's life, just as he does for your own. I'm glad God loves us even though we do not fit into the "perfect people" box, aren't you?

There is also deep pain in not being able to have children of your own. This, too, is an area of great disappointment and grief that many couples face today, and it is easy to lose hope. Waiting on God's timing and watching others with their kids can be a terribly painful road. You may feel as though God doesn't hear your cry for a child. This is a very difficult journey of faith: trusting God even when you don't understand why. Yet God sees your situation and is able to bring something good despite the frustration.

3. Disappointment with Self

Have you ever met a woman who was perfectly satisfied with the way she looks? Me neither! Even the most beautiful of friends complain about their weight or complexion or hair or veins. You name it, there's a lot to whine about when it comes to appearance. But our disappointment with self is not just limited to our bodies; it extends to many different areas of life. We can be disappointed with our emotional weaknesses or our lack of abilities, talents, or strengths. There are times we may become discouraged in the way we handle relationships or our inability to get the right job or our lack of discipline.

A woman is never at a loss for ways to be down on herself. In fact, we are champs at beating ourselves up mentally over past choices or mistakes. Let me assure you, if you struggle in this area, you are definitely not alone. Unfortunately, most women don't reveal their self-disappointment in a typical conversation, and this tends to make us feel as though we are the only ones who are unhappy with the way we turned out. We feel alone when it comes to how we view ourselves; yet if we were to expose every woman's inner communication with self, we would find most of us have an internal struggle with confidence—some of us are just better at hiding it than others. The good news is God works through both our strengths and our weaknesses for a greater purpose.

> *A woman is never at a loss for ways to be down on herself.*

4. Disappointment with Others

It is probably safe to say that someone has let you down at some point in your life. The fact is, even the noblest of people will disappoint us, because we are all human and we are all sinners. Friends will frustrate us, in-laws will annoy us, coworkers will anger us, and neighbors will be unkind to us. It's the painful truth about humanity. If you think you are the only person in the world who has been wounded by another person, think again. People have been causing pain to others since the beginning of time (remember Cain and Abel?).[7] The question is not whether we will be disappointed by others, but how we will handle the disappointments. Will we allow them to grow into bitterness and resentment, or will we live in the realm of grace, forbearance, and forgiveness?

Loneliness can be a by-product of our disappointment with people. It can develop as a result of our own choice to distance ourselves from a hurtful person, or it could be a result of someone distancing herself from us. You may have trouble connecting with people because you have been hurt in the past, or perhaps you have a tendency to be critical of others. Loneliness can be excruciating at times, yet God can comfort us in our loneliness through his presence and through his people. He can also use our loneliness as a catalyst to help us reach out to others and draw closer to God.

5. Disappointment with Circumstances

Do you feel like life is not exactly blowing you kisses? Circumstances beyond your control may have turned your seemingly happy life into a completely different scenario. I'm not sure any of us will ever be comfortable with the fact that situations can dramatically change, sometimes altering our dreams forever. A debilitating injury, a devastating hurricane, an unexpected layoff, an unplanned pregnancy, a cancer diagnosis, bankruptcy, addiction, divorce—all can lead us into lives we did not plan.

Financial disappointments can be a constant source of frustration and pain. Whether it's a downturn in the economy, job loss, or personal mishandling of finances, challenges can arise for people at any income level. You may feel as though you will never get back on your feet again, or you may feel frustrated because you are not living at the level you always thought you would. Although life seems unfair and unpredictable, I want to reassure you it is also full of potential and possibilities. The path you are on right now may not be fun or glamorous, but God can give you strength day by day as you move toward the hope ahead of you.

6. Disappointment with Religion

If you are disillusioned by established religion, you are a part of an increasing number of individuals, both Christian and non-Christian alike. Many young people today don't see the church as a place where Christ's love is exemplified; rather, they view the Christian community as hateful and condemning. Sadly, in many churches, Christ's message of loving others as Christ loves us has faded into haughty attitudes and hateful disputes.

As believers, we need to be a community that shows the world what Christ's love looks like, beginning with the gospel and moving out to touch lives with compassion. The authentic church based on the foundation of Jesus Christ is a beautiful thing. Unfortunately, many have been hurt by religiosity, whether it was a bad experience in a church, a not-so-faithful minister, or cruel students at a Christian school. Gossip, cliques, or judgmental spirits can also cause disillusionment with religion in general. You may have some scars that need God's loving salve. As we take our focus off religion and put it back on Jesus, we begin to see the glory and goodness of his sincere love.

7. Disappointment with God

You prayed and prayed, and no clear answer seemed to come. Or worse, you prayed fervently, passionately, ceaselessly . . . only to have the situation turn out exactly the opposite of what you asked. You thought God loved you and would take care of you, but your life fell apart.

When disappointments like these come into our lives, we find ourselves asking, "Where is God?" Maybe you have shaken your fist at God in anger or given up on him completely. Perhaps you just decided to slowly distance yourself in your relationship with him, because you haven't seen him show up. Disappointment with God comes in many different forms. Usually it brings with it a fair amount of guilt as the Enemy whispers in your ear, *How could you give up on God? What kind of person are you anyway?*

Believe it or not, some of our greatest Christian leaders have had moments of doubt or disillusionment. Even in the Bible we see Job's questioning and David's hopeless feelings. John the Baptist sent a message to Jesus from his dark prison cell asking, "Are you the Messiah we've been expecting, or should we keep looking for someone else?"[8] Often disappointment with God results from not being able to understand God. We can't comprehend that a loving, sovereign God would allow bad things to happen in our lives, so we question whether he is really there or whether he is who he says he is.

As we walk through this book together, I hope you will experience God in a new and fresh way. He can pick up the broken pieces of your life. Understanding why he allowed something in your life will not change the reality of who he is and what he can do through your circumstances. Whether we understand why God allowed something or not, we do know his comfort and care is available to us in the middle of our pain, for Scripture tells us, "The Lord is close to the brokenhearted and saves those who are crushed in spirit."[9]

A Beautiful Weaving of Hope

I'm sure you could relate to at least a few of the disappointments listed in this chapter (okay, maybe more than just a few). The good news is that although our lives haven't turned out like we thought they would, all is not lost. Situations that seem frustrating or difficult could actually turn out to be opportunities to see God's mighty and redeeming hand at work. Although we may not be able to envision the end result, God has a plan that goes far beyond what we can see.

Throughout this book, you will read stories about women just like you and me who have weathered the storms of change in their lives. In every story I hope you will see the hand of God carrying her along through her difficulties and leading her to new possibilities. Yes, God can use the twists and turns in our lives to lead us on a new journey. He may have a greater, eternal purpose that we cannot understand right now, and we may not fully comprehend it until we see Jesus face to face. The question is, are we willing to trust God and believe that he will bring blessings out of our pain? Will we trust him to design a new life that may be more beautiful than we ever imagined? Or will we settle for mere survival, or— maybe even less than survival—will we fall into discouragement, bitterness, and frustration?

Hope in God can turn disappointments into appointments to trust God. As David said in the midst of his sadness, "Why are you downcast, O my soul? Why so disturbed within me? Put your hope in God, for I will yet praise him, my Savior and my God."[10]

Personally, I have found great encouragement from reading the words of the Old Testament prophet Jeremiah, who is known as the "weeping prophet." Can you believe that? Encouragement from the weeping prophet! But I think you will be encouraged too. As Jeremiah grieved over the destruction of Jerusalem, he turned his eyes toward the day-to-day faithfulness of the Lord. Notice how

Jeremiah's discouragement turns into words of strength as he dares to hope.

> The thought of my suffering and homelessness
> is bitter beyond words.
> I will never forget this awful time,
> as I grieve over my loss.
> Yet I still dare to hope
> when I remember this:
>
> The faithful love of the LORD never ends!
> His mercies never cease.
> Great is his faithfulness;
> his mercies begin afresh each morning.
> I say to myself, "The LORD is my inheritance;
> therefore, I will hope in him!"
>
> The LORD is good to those who depend on him,
> to those who search for him.
> So it is good to wait quietly
> for salvation from the LORD."[11]

Will you dare to hope as Jeremiah did? As he grieved his loss, he also declared, "The faithful love of the LORD never ends!" Yes, his mercy is new and fresh each morning. My friend, as you walk this new and different road, seek God's goodness and mercy along the way. Cry out to him for help, and trust his faithfulness to get you through one day at a time. Not one of us has been guaranteed a perfectly happy life. The Bible reminds us, "The righteous person faces many troubles, but the LORD comes to the rescue each time."[12]

We will experience challenges in life, but God will not leave us. We may be called to persevere through trials and be patient in tribulation, but God can still bring hope. Perhaps you have wondered, *Doesn't God want me to be happy? Surely he doesn't want me to be miserable.* The truth is, our hearts long for a lovely and happy life. We long for heaven. The Bible doesn't promise us perfect circumstances here on earth, but it does offer us the opportunity to experience peace and joy through Christ.

One of my favorite passages in the Bible is found in the book of Nehemiah. God's people had just returned to Jerusalem and had gathered together to hear the reading of the Book of the Law of God. As they stood there listening to God's words, they began weeping. Their hearts moved toward repentance as they opened their hearts to God. Nehemiah encouraged them, "Don't be dejected and sad, for the joy of the LORD is your strength!"[13]

As we turn our hearts toward the Lord, his joy can be our strength as well. It is not a joy brought on by our circumstances or by people; it is a deeper joy that comes from the Lord. Jesus said, "When you obey my commandments, you remain in my love, just as I obey my Father's commandments and remain in his love. I have told you these things so that you will be filled with my joy. Yes, your joy will overflow!"[14] Certainly God wants us to experience an overflowing joy, a joy that comes from abiding in him and walking in his ways. Life may not always be happy, but the joy of the Lord can always be our strength.

> *Life may not always be happy, but the joy of the Lord can always be our strength.*

Hope and *joy* are two words that seem to be woven into the life of Corrie ten Boom. Although she spent ten months in a Nazi concentration camp during World War II and suffered the loss of four of her family members as a result of their hiding Jewish people from the Gestapo, she had a strength that could only come from the Lord. Here is a poem she often quoted as a result of experiencing God's hand at work in her life.

The Weaver

by Grant Colfax Tuller (1869–1950)

My life is but a weaving
Between my Lord and me;
I cannot choose the colors
He worketh steadily.
Oft' times He weaveth sorrow;
And I, in foolish pride,
Forget He sees the upper,
And I the underside.
Not 'til the loom is silent
And the shuttles cease to fly,
Will God unroll the canvas
And reveal the reason why.
The dark threads are as needful
In the Weaver's skillful hand,
As the threads of gold and silver
In the pattern He has planned.
He knows, He loves, He cares;
Nothing this truth can dim.
He gives the very best to those
Who choose to walk with Him.

Corrie added, "We see the back of the embroidery, God sees the front! He knows how beautiful it will be."[15] The circumstances of your life may not look pretty right now. There are times you will feel afraid or as though there is no hope. But God has not left you. He has a plan he is weaving together in his faithfulness and love. Wait and watch, my friend. Continue to seek God's help and ask him for his hope to fill your heart. The Weaver of your life has not finished his work in you. The life you didn't plan may lead you to a new purpose and passion in which you will joyfully *thrive*.

STEPPING FORWARD

 ### POINTS

- You are not alone. God is with you in the midst of your discouraging circumstances.
- Every woman has experienced disappointments to some degree in her life.
- The following are the seven most common disappointments in women's lives.
    1. Disappointment with marriage
    2. Disappointment with kids
    3. Disappointment with self
    4. Disappointment with others
    5. Disappointment with circumstances
    6. Disappointment with religion
    7. Disappointment with God
- Every disappointment can be turned into an appointment to trust God's plan.
- Dare to place your hope in God.
- Great is God's faithfulness! Day by day we can experience his mercy and joy as we turn our eyes toward him.
- God is a redeeming God who is weaving a greater, more eternal picture than what we can see right now.

 ### PASSAGE: PSALM 139:7–18

I can never escape from your Spirit!
    I can never get away from your presence!
If I go up to heaven, you are there;
    if I go down to the grave, you are there.

If I ride the wings of the morning,
    if I dwell by the farthest oceans,
even there your hand will guide me,
    and your strength will support me.
I could ask the darkness to hide me
    and the light around me to become night—
    but even in darkness I cannot hide from you.
To you the night shines as bright as day.
    Darkness and light are the same to you.

You made all the delicate, inner parts of my body
    and knit me together in my mother's womb.
Thank you for making me so wonderfully complex!
    Your workmanship is marvelous—how well I know it.
You watched me as I was being formed in utter seclusion,
    as I was woven together in the dark of the womb.
You saw me before I was born.
    Every day of my life was recorded in your book.
Every moment was laid out
    before a single day had passed.

How precious are your thoughts about me, O God.
    They cannot be numbered!
I can't even count them;
    they outnumber the grains of sand!
And when I wake up,
    you are still with me!

 PRAYER

Gracious and kind heavenly Father, I praise you for your loving presence. Although I cannot understand why disappointments happen in my life, I can trust that you will love me and be with me to see me through. I know you will redeem my disappointment; thank you for using the difficulties and challenges in my life to help me grow stronger. Thank you for the strength you give me through the process. I believe you have a bigger plan I cannot see. Help me to walk by faith and not by sight. I love you, Lord. In Jesus' name, amen.

 ## PLAN

Consider the disappointments you are currently experiencing in life. Take a moment to write them down in a notebook or even in the back of this book. Now prayerfully go over each disappointment, asking God to comfort you and give you strength and hope. Write down the following verse, Zephaniah 3:17 NIV, on an index card, and memorize it as you journey through this unexpected path.

The Lord your God is with you,
    he is mighty to save.
He will take great delight in you,
    he will quiet you with his love,
    he will rejoice over you with singing.

Our troubles have always brought us blessings,
and they always will.
They are the black chariots of bright grace.

C. H. Spurgeon

2

Time to Let Go

*Climbing Out of Your Rut
and Moving On with Your Life*

The LORD *is close to the brokenhearted;
he rescues those whose spirits are crushed.*

Psalm 34:18

Jennifer Griffin thought she was experiencing a common stomach virus when she couldn't seem to keep anything down. But on the third day of the unpleasant symptoms, Jennifer was so weak she couldn't even stand up. Her husband of only five months suspected a dangerous level of dehydration and called an ambulance. Neither thought the situation was terribly serious, but by the time she arrived at the emergency room, it was obvious that something was terribly wrong. Jennifer remembers, "It seems like it was only twenty minutes from the time I arrived until I was being rolled into surgery."

What happened next was so dramatic it seems almost like something you would see in a Hollywood movie. The doctors discovered that an abscess on Jennifer's ovary had ruptured, and toxic infection was ravaging her body. The diagnosis: sepsis and multiorgan failure. Doctors immediately began fighting to save her life. Jennifer was surrounded by family and friends who rallied around her with love and support. Slowly Jennifer began to get better, but part of her did not. You see, the body naturally draws blood from the extremities to fight infections in the internal organs, so although Jennifer survived, her hands and feet did not.

Jennifer's hands were amputated just below the wrist and her legs at midcalf. Amazingly, Jennifer considers herself lucky, "I got to keep my knees and my wrists; it's really the best of a worst situation." Jennifer, who had always lived an active lifestyle, has become an inspiration and marvel to all who know her. Now, less than a year later, she zips around on prosthetic legs that she lovingly named Fred Astaire and Ginger Rogers. She has learned to drive and type again, and she has returned to her job as a corporate paralegal.

Her husband, Nick, is incredibly proud of her attitude and strength. He said, "I expected an emotional roller coaster, but I can honestly say there has never been a single moment when Jen said, 'Why did this happen to me?' I haven't seen one second of self-pity." Jennifer did interject, "Oh, I absolutely have moments. It's not self-pity, but simple frustration when I'm trying to do something like pick up a glass and it slips through my hands."

Jennifer says she lives a richer, happier life than ever. "Honestly, in my heart of hearts, I don't know why this freaky thing happened, but I wouldn't change it," she said. "So much has happened in our lives, I wouldn't change it. . . . I honestly feel there is a reason for it."

Jennifer has gone on to start a foundation called P.L.A.Y. (Positive Living for Active Youth), which assists young amputees to become involved with sports activities as a way to build their self-esteem and confidence. (Check it out at www.PlayFoundation.net.) You will have to agree Jennifer is an amazing individual who has certainly learned how to thrive, not simply survive, in the life she didn't plan. She made a conscious choice to accept what she had rather than wallow in self-pity about what was taken from her.[1]

Jennifer's story is a dramatic one. Although you may not have experienced a physical setback of such magnitude, you have had setbacks in your life, I'm sure. Your disappointment, whether big or small, is very real to you. I provided Jennifer's story not for you to compare yourself with her, but rather for you to be encouraged and inspired by her acceptance of her circumstances and her desire to journey down the road to recovery with a positive outlook. The road of life is speckled with unexpected potholes, some of them quite deep, and we must decide whether to stay in a rut or begin to move on.

In a Rut

Are you stuck? I mean emotionally stuck, grieving or frustrated by the way things turned out. Getting stuck can happen to any of us, often without our even recognizing it. We may be traveling delightfully along life's pathway, when—*boom!*—things change, and we must adjust. When our hearts sink at the loss of a dream, we can be deeply saddened because things didn't turn out as we thought they should or would. We can grope through a wide range of feelings such as frustration, disappointment, anger, and grief.

We must adequately face our grief, but we must also accept our new set of circumstances and begin to move on. How do we move through grief and toward acceptance? Most of us have never taken a course in "How to Handle Disappointment." We simply stumble through the emotions and pain, hoping to find joy once again. In this chapter, I want us to consider some practical ways to move through your disappointments and climb out of your rut.

Ask yourself the following questions (you may even want to ask a trusted friend to give you her honest opinion of what she sees in you):

- Are your thoughts constantly consumed with your disappointment?
- Do you continue to rehash the situation over and over again in conversations?
- Are you holding a grudge against the person who hurt you?

- Do you keep playing the if-only-this-hadn't-happened scenario in your mind?
- Are you savoring a poor-me mentality?
- Do you repeatedly tell people who are trying to help you, "You just don't know how hard my life is"? (Exception: If you are in an abusive situation, be honest. Get help and tell a counselor or friend how bad it is immediately.)

If you identified yourself in any of these statements, you may be stuck, but you can move forward. I know it has been hard and you must grieve over your loss, but there comes a time when you need to climb out of your sadness and grief and move on. Honestly, it is easy to wallow in a rut without recognizing it. Some people stay there because they like playing the victim role. Others enjoy the attention they get from their sad story. Many people stay in a rut simply because they don't recognize they have fallen into it, and they haven't thought about how to get out. They just don't know how to take a first step toward happiness again.

> *There comes a time when you need to climb out of your sadness and grief and move on.*

Good Grief

It is healthy and good to recognize when we are experiencing heartbreak or disappointment. Most of us think of grief in terms of the death of a loved one, but if we are honest with ourselves, a certain amount of grief hits us when the path we are on suddenly changes. Now, certainly it is not the same type of grief that is experienced with the loss of a loved one, but it is grief just the same. It hurts when our dreams die or our plans perish. When things turn out differently than we thought they would or could, we may experience an emotional letdown or pain. We take a positive step forward when we accept the honest fact that we are sad over the loss.

I also want to mention there are times in our lives when we may even come to a place of complete brokenness. We can be broken in our realization of our own sin, or we may be broken emotionally or physically, feeling as though we are not able to move in our own power and strength. When we are broken, we begin to look upward and see our need for God. In Psalms, we read, "He [the Lord] heals the brokenhearted and binds up their wounds."[2] Through our poverty and brokenness, God gently begins a cleansing process, and he lovingly puts us back together again.

A woman who is passionately living the life she didn't plan doesn't wear an "I'm Invincible" badge. Even Jennifer admitted her feelings of frustration. We must be honest about how we feel and not try to candy-coat our situation or ignore our emotions. If we repress our feelings, we may be in danger of exploding or imploding later down the road. We can be authentic and real as well as courageous and strong. Cry if you need to. Find solace in God's Word, in prayer, in journaling, and in talking with a friend, a mentor, or a counselor. Don't try to hide your pain just because you want to present a tough-girl, I-can-handle-it image.

> *We can be authentic and real as well as courageous and strong.*

A word of caution: there is a big difference between grieving a loss and continually whining and complaining about our circumstances. Grumbling goes beyond telling someone about your disappointment; it moves into the category of actively (and possibly angrily) retelling your story over and over again. It may include a good measure of self-pity as well, which is quite unbecoming of any woman. Helen Keller said, "Self-pity is our worst enemy and if we yield to it, we can never do anything wise in this world."[3] Blind and deaf since early childhood, if anyone had an excuse to whine and complain, it was Helen Keller; yet she chose to see a life of possibilities despite her physical disabilities.

Let's decide to steer clear of whining, complaining, and self-pity. We don't want to ignore the sadness we feel, but we don't want to cuddle up with our sadness either. The important thing is to identify our sorrow and then begin moving forward. Grieve, yes; stay there, no. When we find ourselves on Heartbreak Hill, we don't have to set up camp. If we are going to thrive, we must leave the pity-party behind us.

> *"Self-pity is our worst enemy and if we yield to it, we can never do anything wise in this world."*
> —*Helen Keller*

Accept the Challenge

One of the most memorable trips we have taken as a family was to the hill country of Texas back when our daughters were in middle school. We decided to explore a state park with a unique giant rock formation called Enchanted Rock. As we watched other hikers ascend the mount, we felt compelled to do the same. Within minutes we were a vigorously climbing family machine, and we reached the top in no time. What victory! We had proudly conquered the mountain (okay, mount). And the view was breathtaking! We were able to see the beautiful Texas hill country for miles and miles in every direction.

Soon it began to rain, and we realized it was time to descend the amazing mount. Did I mention that Enchanted Rock is a rather large *smooth* rock? Somehow it was not a problem getting up, but with the rain and the steep slope, it was a big problem getting down. We took it slowly, methodically, and carefully. We recognized that one little slip could send us into an injury-laden fall. We found a less steep path on the other side of the mount, and Curt helped each of the kids as we crossed over difficult spots. We were elated when we finally touched horizontal ground.

Although the descent was rather challenging, it turned out to be a good experience. It was an opportunity for the four of us to depend on one another for support and encouragement along the way. Getting down the mount safely was truly a much sweeter victory than making it to the top.

The point is, we had to get down from that mount. It wasn't easy, and we had to help one another, but we made it. You may find yourself in a situation you didn't plan. Just as it was necessary for us as a family to carefully make our way down the steep slopes of Enchanted Rock, so you will need to deliberately and carefully push forward past the grief. You may attempt to dwell on what the future holds, but don't go there. Just take one step at a time, day by day, hour by hour, with the Lord as your guide and strength and the people he has put in your life as your encouragers.

Accepting your situation is your first and most important mental step as you work through your disappointments. It is easy to become trapped in the rut of blaming others for your predicaments or continually whining about what has happened. Some people become consumed with the question, "Why did God allow this to happen to me?" There is a point where you must simply accept what has happened and begin dealing with it. You may never know why it happened, and it doesn't help your situation to continue to blame others. It's time to say, "Here I am in this place. Now how am I going to make the best of it?"

> *Accepting your situation is your first and most important mental step as you work through your disappointments.*

Let's take a look at what two women from the Old Testament can teach us about dealing with disappointment in a positive way.

Recognize the Disappointment

In the book of Ruth, we are introduced to a sorrowful situation of a woman named Naomi. Imagine Naomi's indescribable pain of not only suffering the death of her spouse, but then also experiencing the death of not one but *both* of her sons. Suddenly widowed and childless, Naomi saw her dream of a large, happy family with lots of grandkids washed away in a sea of sorrow. I'm sure she felt as though her life was over and she would never experience happiness again. The only inkling of good she had in her life was her daughter-in-law Ruth, who chose to stay with her. Yet Naomi had something else going for her—she was honest about the way she felt.

When Ruth and Naomi returned to Naomi's hometown of Bethlehem after the terrible loss of their husbands, they were greeted with excitement by the people in the town. "Is it really Naomi?" the women asked. Naomi didn't try to play the "I'm Invincible" game. She said, "Don't call me Naomi [which means pleasant]. . . . Call me Mara [which means bitter], for the Almighty has made life very bitter for me. I went away full, but the LORD has brought me home empty. Why call me Naomi when the LORD has caused me to suffer and the Almighty has sent such tragedy upon me?"[4]

Naomi told it like it was. She didn't hide her hurt. I'm embarrassed to tell you I used to read the book of Ruth and think in my arrogant little way that Naomi was depressed and needed to get over it. I thought, *God was with her, and he gave her Ruth as a companion and later made her the great-grandmother of King David, so what's the problem?* Easy for me to say, for I knew the outcome of the story. Poor Naomi was in the middle of grief in the first chapter of Ruth. She had every right to be hurting, and I believe she offers us a poignant example of honesty in recognizing and grieving life's disappointments. The good news is, she didn't stay there. She let go of her old dream and moved forward.

In the same way, we need to steer clear of pretending we aren't hurt or ignoring the fact that we feel pain. We don't have to go around advertising it or informing every person we see, but we do need to be open with the people who care about us. We don't need to wallow in our pain; we simply need to be honest that we have it. Think about it this way: do we try to minister to others who are hurting by showing them our steel-plated emotional armor or by opening up fellowship through shared sufferings?

Solomon reminds us, "For everything there is a season, a time for every activity under heaven. . . . A time to cry and a time to laugh. A time to grieve and a time to dance."[5] Jesus wept, David grieved, and we must walk through our emotions as well. "Don't sidestep suffering," says Katherine Anne Porter. "You have to go through it to get where you're going."[6] Allow grief to take its course, knowing that you won't be in this place forever. Consciously let go of the old dream as you look to God to lead you to the next chapter in your life.

See God's Care

God sent a provision for Naomi's life in the form of her daughter-in-law Ruth. Certainly Ruth also had reason to grieve as her husband had died as well, leaving her and her mother-in-law with no means of income. Ruth began to look for a glimmer of hope and found it! Although not an Israelite herself, she knew that the Jewish law required the landowners to leave certain sections of their fields unharvested, and any grain that was dropped by the harvesters was to be left on the ground for the poor to gather. You see, many years earlier, God had set in place a provision for people in need.

What has God provided for you? It may be a helping hand or the listening ear of a friend. It may be a counselor at your church or a group of women at Bible study. It may be a physical provision of some sort. It may be God's presence and peace. The Bible reminds us that God is our Keeper and our Provider. The apostle Paul from his prison cell said, "This same God who takes care of me will supply all your needs from his glorious riches, which have been given to us in Christ Jesus."[7]

Let's open our eyes to the care God is giving us. We can begin by turning our eyes toward what we can be grateful for and turning our focus away from all that is awful. Consider keeping a "Thank you, God" journal as you walk your road of disappointment. Each day write down at least one provision God has given you, and thank him for it. It may be as simple as God's provision of food for that day or a roof over your head or a friend who called to ask you how you are doing.

Giving thanks ought to be a continual practice in our lives when things are going well and when things stink. Even on our most difficult days, there is at least something (even if it is small) for which we can be thankful. Putting an entry into a "Thank you, God" journal every day helps us slowly turn from our sadness and begin to see possibilities. It forces us to observe what God has done and find reassurance of what he can do.

A friend of mine, Denise Waters, felt compelled to write down at least five things she was thankful for every day. This attitude of gratitude so transformed her life and her way of thinking that she even created a guided journal called *Give Thanks 5 a Day*, which has a place each day to write five things for which you are grateful. She made mugs and magnets, too, as daily reminders to continually give God thanks. Isn't that great? Try the principles of giving thanks each day, and you will find it will begin to transform your thinking as well. Most important, it will help you open your eyes to God's care and the way he is working in your life day by day.

If you are having trouble seeing anything good about your life right now, I encourage you to ask a friend to help you recognize even some small things to be thankful for in your circumstances. The good things are there, but sometimes we become so focused on our frustrations that we are not able to see the good. So ask a friend or family member to jump-start your list of gratitude, and then continue on your own. I know you will experience a lift in your attitude and spirit.

Create a New Plan

Thankfully, Ruth and Naomi didn't stay in their pit of despair. They saw God's provision and took a step toward hope. Hope shed light on a new plan. Ruth had found favor with the landowner Boaz. In his providence, God led Ruth to a field where she not only received care, but also had an opportunity. Boaz was Naomi's relative and therefore had the responsibility to take care of widowed family members. Naomi saw the glimmer of hope and created a plan. She instructed Ruth to get all cleaned up and pretty and go to the threshing floor where Boaz could be found.

Ruth listened to Naomi and stepped forward in faith, carefully and humbly approaching Boaz as her "kinsman redeemer." Many years before, God made a provision for widows through their kinsmen. The kinsman redeemer was to take care of or marry those in his family who were widowed. God provided for Ruth and Naomi, but they had to take some steps of action.

> *Don't worry about three days from now or how you are going to spend future holidays; just take one step forward.*

What are your possibilities? Can you see a potential new plan of action as a way of adjusting to the changes from your original plan? Maybe you will need to get a job or find a new place to live, or perhaps you must find a different school for the special needs of your child. Prayerfully ask God to open your eyes to your next steps. Seek his guidance as he leads you along the path you should go. Don't worry about three days from now or how you are going to spend future holidays; just take one step toward the direction in which he is leading you right now.

Pray honestly and expectantly as you seek God's direction. The opposite of seeking God's direction is pridefully forging ahead on our own. It's so easy to do! Many of us tend to want to push forward with our ideas, thinking we have it all figured out. This go-getter, gotta-make-it-happen mentality so easily slips into our way of living and dealing with challenges. Let's choose to spend time seeking God's direction first and then humbly taking those first steps forward. You may not have the whole plan figured out, but follow God's leading as he opens doors and provides opportunities. He provides guidance through his Word, through wise counsel, and even through circumstances.

Part of the new plan may also include letting go of the need to get back at someone or to make things fair. Are you willing to trust God to bring justice to the situation? We will talk more specifically about forgiveness in chapter 6. God may not lead you down an easy path, and you may need to trust him step by step, but he will never leave you or forsake you. He will be walking alongside you as you step into a new plan. As the saying goes, "Where God guides, he provides."

Take Your Eyes off the Past

As we begin to climb out of the rut and step forward to what God has ahead, it is important for us to take our focus off past hurts and mistakes. Thoughts and reminders of your pain or disappointment or how things could have been will pop into your head now and then. It's time to leave the regrets behind and turn your eyes toward what God is planning for the rest of your life.

The apostle Paul offers us a good example. He could have chosen to live in his past, wallowing in regret about his former years of persecuting Christians, but he chose to look forward.

Here's what he said to the Philippians: "I focus on this one thing: Forgetting the past and looking forward to what lies ahead, I press on to reach the end of the race and receive the heavenly prize for which God, through Christ Jesus, is calling us."[8]

Jesus himself used an example about not looking back as he spoke about the coming of the kingdom of God, saying, "Remember what happened to Lot's wife!"[9] Do you remember Lot's wife? She was the woman in the Old Testament who turned into a pillar of salt because she looked back at her old life going up in smoke. Now I don't think God is going to turn us into pillars of salt if we glance back down memory lane, but I do think we stagnate if we continue to hold on to old dreams when it is time to move on. If we get stuck in the mode of holding on to our pasts, we are ineffective for the here and now.

> *We stagnate if we continue to hold on to old dreams when it is time to move on.*

Whether you are dealing with a divorce or an injury or a loss, you have a choice: you can dwell on what could have been and your past dreams, or you can remember Lot's wife and move forward to what is next. One "talent" we have as women is to replay the "I'm Hurt" tape over and over in our minds. *They hurt my feelings. He ruined my life. She was rude to me. God didn't listen to me.* Once you have grieved a hurt or loss, it is time to stop reliving the hurt and replaying the video over and over in your mind. Again, this requires forgiveness, but we have a loving God who is able to give us the strength to forgive. Seek his help when you just can't get to the place of forgiveness.

The only time Scripture tells us to look back is when we are remembering what God has done. The Israelites were told to set up markers and memorials to remember what God had brought them through. We, too, must reflect on God's goodness and recognize all he has done, instead of reflecting on our past life and wishing it were still there. To passionately live the life we didn't plan, we must turn our eyes upward instead of backward in order to go forward.

The Power of Looking Up

Missionary David Miner Stern was plunged into deep grief at the death of his young daughter. Try as he might, David could not seem to get over his great sorrow, even though he was a Christian and knew of the Lord's care. In his depression, he visited his daughter's grave every day. He had a walking stick that he used to touch the mound of dirt over her casket, and somehow this seemed to give him a small measure of comfort, as it made him feel as though he had some slight contact with her. The oppression of his grief was so severe that he feared he must give up his role as a missionary. But God in his gracious way brought him relief.

One day as he stood over the grave, David suddenly realized how wrong it was for him to fix his attention on the dead body of his daughter. The Holy Spirit began to impress on his mind what Jesus said to the thief as he was dying on the cross: "Today you will be with me in paradise."[10] The truth of the passage began to transform the way he was thinking and he started repeating the words "with Christ in paradise" over and over again as he walked home.

His mind opened up to the blessed reality of his daughter being with Jesus. He asked himself, "What more could I want for a loved one than this?" This comforting thought allowed him to resume his missionary duties with joy. Instead of dwelling on his daughter in the grave, he pictured her safe in the presence of Jesus.[11]

By God's grace and power, we, too, can see our circumstances in a different way. It's time to let go of that old dream and walk hand in hand with the Lord into a new and different place. With our eyes looking up, we are able to catch a glimpse of a better dream. Most important, as we look to Christ, we are reminded of his great and comforting love, which can soothe the pain and give us strength to move forward.

STEPPING FORWARD

POINTS

- Grieve the loss of a dream, but do not stay in that grief.
- Self-pity, complaining, whining, and grumbling have no redeeming value.
- Allow God to comfort you in your brokenness.
- Recognize the disappointment, and experience the grief.
- See God's care, and thank him for his provision.
- Create a new plan, and take one step forward.
- Take your eyes off the past, and stop reviewing your hurt.

PASSAGE: HABAKKUK 3:17–19

Even though the fig trees have no blossoms,
    and there are no grapes on the vines;
even though the olive crop fails,
    and the fields lie empty and barren;
even though the flocks die in the fields,
    and the cattle barns are empty,
yet I will rejoice in the LORD!
    I will be joyful in the God of my salvation!
The Sovereign LORD is my strength!
    He makes me as surefooted as a deer,
    able to tread upon the heights.

PRAYER

Glorious and loving heavenly Father, you are my strength when I am weak and my hope when all seems lost. When I am in despair, you know my pain and you see my sorrow. Help me work through my grief. Hold me while I cry. Please dry my tears, and lead me toward a new plan. Guide my steps. Oh Father, help me to forgive, as you are the great Forgiver. Keep my focus on you, and don't let me dwell on the past. My desire is to move forward with you as you lead me and even carry me when necessary. Thank you, Lord, for your never-ending presence in my life. In Jesus' name, amen.

PLAN

1. Write down several words that describe your personal discouragement or grief.

   _____

   _____

   _____

   _____

   _____

   _____

   _____

2. Take a moment to pray and tell God how you feel. Ask for his healing and help.

3. Write down at least one way you see God's help in your life right now and thank him for it.

   _____

4. Seek his guidance in one step you can take to move forward.

5. Write down one step (even if it is a small one) you will take to move forward.

_____

_____

_____

When will you take that first step? _____

Worry is a thin stream of fear trickling though the mind.
If encouraged, it cuts a channel into which
all other thoughts are drained.

Arthur Somers Roche

3

Worry and What-Ifs

Conquering the Anxieties and Fears
That Dominate Your Mind

I prayed to the LORD, and he answered me.
He freed me from all my fears.
Those who look to him for help will be radiant with joy;
No shadow of shame will darken their faces.

Psalm 34:4–5

Jane and her husband, Mark, waited for the doctor to come into the pre-op room to address them before surgery. It was to be a normal hysterectomy, and it was about time. Jane had weathered years of "female issues" and pain, so at the age of forty-five, she was simply ready to get rid of the plumbing! Mark and Jane had a beautiful ten-year-old daughter, and although they had tried for years to have more children, they recognized it was time to move on with their lives and be thankful for what God had given them.

As Jane lay on the gurney in the pre-op room, the doctor walked in and said, "Well, I have good news and I have bad news. The bad news is I can't do this surgery. The good news is you are pregnant." Pregnant at forty-five! Just when Jane and Mark thought they had life figured out, they entered into a life they didn't plan. Of course Jane and Mark were ecstatic, but they did have their concerns.

What were the health risks for a midlife woman having a baby? What were the risks for the baby? How would she have the energy to take care of a newborn? What would it be like for Mark and Jane to watch their child graduate from high school when they were in their sixties? What would it be like for the child to have older parents? Mark and Jane had also figured out their budget for the next umpteen years—and a new baby and another college education had not figured into the picture. Their heads were swimming with many what-ifs and worries.

Mark and Jane realized this was an opportunity to trust God. They walked in faith, praying continually for God's watchful care over Jane's and the baby's health. The pregnancy and delivery went well, and now they are the proud parents of precious little Luke. Jane has had a tremendous sense of humor and a positive attitude throughout the whole adventure. She has jumped back into being the mother of a preschooler with joy and expectation. Jane, who is an author, has also been a tremendous source of encouragement to many other midlife moms.[1]

Jane says, "Although this is not the life we planned, we could not be happier with our healthy, happy, joy-filled little miracle boy. We still look at him and wonder when his parents are coming to pick him up. In life, flexibility is paramount. We thank God for Luke as we ask God for wisdom in all the new decisions we are making every day." As far as the worries about the future, they have continued to trust God and see his hand at work.

Baby Luke was a surprise to Mark and Jane, but he was no surprise to God. God has an exciting plan for Luke as well as a new chapter in his mommy's and daddy's lives.

Uncertainties pop up in happy circumstances as well as tragic ones, and worry can tend to dominate our thinking if we let it. As women who desire to passionately live the life we didn't plan, we must make a deliberate choice to move away from a pattern of worry, and focus instead on the inklings of hope God provides along the way. We have no guarantee that our situation will turn out exactly as we want it to. The only fact we can be assured of is God's presence, no matter what happens.

Worry versus Responsibility

When life brings about unexpected changes, we tend to experience anxiety and despair. The fear of the unknown breeds worry quicker than you can say, "How in the world did I get here?" Personally speaking, given any circumstance, I can think about all the negative possibilities and scenarios that could play out. What about you? Do you ever start thinking, *What if this happens?* Let's be honest—many of us are quite gifted at dwelling on the negative possibilities in our brains. It's amazing how much time and brain power we waste in wondering and fear.

> *It's amazing how much time and brain power we waste in wondering and fear.*

What are you worried about right now? Think about it for a moment. You may be worried about how to discipline your kids or how you are going to tell your husband about the dent in the car or where you are going to go for vacation. Or perhaps you are worried about much grander life issues such as how you are going to pay next month's rent, or how you will care for an elderly parent or help a friend whose child has just been diagnosed with cancer. Anxieties come in all different shapes and sizes, and most of them are born out of a true concern.

Although worrisome thoughts pop into our heads continually, we don't need to allow them to stay there and grow into full-fledged fear. We can actually use the initial angst as a catalyst to begin thinking about our next steps and to start the problem-solving process. Proper planning is often a result of a healthy concern about a potentially difficult situation. A change in circumstances, an unexpected challenge, or a disrupted plan can be the incubator for *responsible decisions* or *stressful anxiety*. We get to choose which one we will allow to grow.

Quite frankly, some people lean so far to the extreme of not worrying that they throw away all reasoning. Let me give you an example. Tina's (not her real name) husband just won't work. He has had several odd jobs, but he would rather sit around all day

Some people lean so far to the extreme of not worrying that they throw away all reasoning.

reading and playing games on the computer. Tina works full-time, but she can't make enough to support her family. Bills are piling up, but her husband's response is, "Don't worry; we just need to trust God." Obviously, he has a faulty concept of trusting God and living without worry. His worry-free-living campaign is just an excuse for irresponsibility.

Tina, on the other hand, is consumed with worry. She is overwhelmed by the bills and fears for her family's future. Her anxiety is at such a high level that her thoughts and conversations are dominated by worry, anger, and frustration. Although she is the responsible one of the two, she is having a difficult time seeing any hope or solutions. And giving her fear to the Lord is the last thing she wants to do, because she sees where her husband's example has gotten them and feels like she would be relinquishing responsibility if she released her worry to God. Tina's mind is closed to possibilities and solutions as she lives in the darkness of fear and lost hope.

You would be surprised how many households are similar in some respects to Tina's. As one spouse leans toward a lack of responsibility, the other moves further into a frantic mode of worry and tension. I use the two extremes in Tina's home to illustrate the necessity of finding a place of reasonable concern and positive actions in the center of difficult circumstances. How do we take our tendency to worry and turn it into an opportunity to move forward?

Dominating Thoughts

Worry is an anxious and fretful state of mind built on assumptions about what could happen in a given situation. On the other hand, responsibility is a healthy concern about circumstances or situations that leads to positive steps of action. Responsibility and careful planning grow into anxiety when fear dominates our thoughts. As we face fresh challenges, we have the opportunity to decide whether we will walk in wisdom or drown in a sea of anxiety.

Consider Jesus' words about worry in his famous Sermon on the Mount: "Don't worry about these things, saying, 'What will we eat? What will we drink? What will we wear?' These things dominate the thoughts of unbelievers, but your heavenly Father already knows all your needs. Seek the Kingdom of God above all else, and live righteously, and he will give you everything you need. So don't worry about tomorrow, for tomorrow will bring its own worries. Today's trouble is enough for today."[2]

Notice Jesus described worry as "dominat[ing] the thoughts of unbelievers." But as followers of Christ, we have a different option than to allow fear and anxiety to take over our hearts and minds. We can seek God and look to him for our provision. We can also recognize that although we may make our plans, the final results are up to our loving God. When people face difficult times, the difference between

> *Throughout the Bible we find great warriors of God who started out as great worriers.*

those who follow Christ and those who don't know him is that the Christ followers have the opportunity to experience a peace and comfort in trusting a loving God. Hmm . . . do you think the world sees an evidence of our trust in God? Or does the world see us dominated by our fears, just like everyone else?

Throughout the Bible we find great *warriors* of God who started out as great *worriers.* Yet in each case we see the same answer to their worries. Just as Jesus told us in the Sermon on the Mount, the cure for worry is to seek him, trust him, and abide in him. Realistically that's not easy to do. Have you ever found yourself saying any of the following?

- "I can't do it! I don't have what it takes."
- "I'm overwhelmed! How can I accomplish this?"
- "I'm scared! I don't know what is going to happen."

Let's visit three examples in the Bible where these same worries surfaced and see what God wants to teach us about our own tendencies to worry.

"I Can't Do It!"—Fighting Feelings of Inadequacy

Travel with me back to the Old Testament. The place is Mount Sinai, which the Bible calls the mountain of God. Moses draws close to a burning bush, and there he encounters a holy God. God directs Moses to go back to Egypt, talk to Pharaoh, and lead the Israelites out of Egypt. What was Moses' response? "Who am I to appear before Pharaoh? Who am I to lead the people of Israel out of Egypt?" God reassuringly answers him, "I will be with you."[3]

When is the last time you felt like God was leading you to do something you didn't think you could do? Or perhaps you were pushed into circumstances for which you did not feel equipped. As our lives take unexpected turns, we, too, can listen to his gentle yet strong voice saying, "I will be with you." Now, it would be lovely if those words completely eliminated all our feelings of inadequacy, wouldn't it? Unfortunately, negative thoughts and what-ifs may still seep into our thought life even when we know God is with us.

Moses struggled with worry, as we see when he continued to make excuses to God. "What if they won't believe me, or listen to me? What if they say, 'The LORD never appeared to you'?"[4] Moses was thinking up some good ones, wasn't he? He was almost as good as you and I in conjuring up opportunities to worry. God responded by showing his power through transforming Moses' wooden staff into a live snake and then back again, as well as making his hand leprous and then healthy again.

Even after witnessing these amazing miracles firsthand, Moses still pleaded with the Lord, "O Lord, I'm not very good with words. I never have been, and I'm not now, even though you have spoken to me. I get tongue-tied, and my words get tangled."[5] Moses may have been questioning God because this is not the plan Moses had for his life. Not so different than what we think sometimes, right? We may protest, "But I've never been good at . . ." or "I always thought I would be . . ." Sometimes God calls us to a new territory and a task that stretches our abilities, and it isn't the safe plan we had in mind. Yet it is often when we are taken out of our comfort zone that we can see God at work far beyond what we can do on our own.

> *When we are taken out of our comfort zone, we can often see God at work far beyond what we can do on our own.*

God responded to Moses' plea of inadequacy by saying, "Who makes a person's mouth? Who decides whether people speak or do not speak, hear or do not hear, see or do not see? Is it not I, the LORD? Now go! I will be with you as you speak, and I will instruct you in what to say."[6] Again we hear God's reassurance of his presence, and this time he encourages Moses by letting him know he will guide him. Dear sister, do you believe the God who made you can equip you for the road ahead, even if it is an unpleasant road? Throughout Scripture we are reminded that God is able to give us "hind's feet for high places."[7] In other words, God makes us sure-footed on our new journeys with him, just as he equips deer to scale rocky, treacherous mountains.

Now, you would think that after God gave Moses reassurance after reassurance, Moses would be ready to take on the task in front of him. Nope! He continued to plead, "Lord, please! Send anyone else."[8] At this point, God became angry with Moses and told him he would send along his brother, Aaron, too. The good news is, after all Moses' worrying, God still used Moses in a powerful and significant way. Moses didn't stay in a rut of worry. He moved forward in faith, and with each step forward, his faith increased.

What can we learn from Moses and his big worries? Sure, Moses struggled with feelings of inadequacy, but he told God about his fears. Then he chose to move forward in faith one step at a time. In the same way, when we are consumed with feelings of inadequacy or when we feel as though the task is too much for us, let's listen to God's gentle voice saying, *I am with you. I made you and will give you everything you need.* Once we are focused on God's presence, we can tell him our worries.

As we give our worries to God, we must still step forward in faith. Moses went from a worrier to a man used by God, and he is considered one of the great fathers of our faith. Don't be discouraged by your worries; give them to God, and continue to step forward in faith—one step at a time—and then watch what God can do.

I love what David wrote in the Psalms about the importance and benefits of trusting God:

Trust in the LORD and do good.
    Then you will live safely in the land and prosper.
Take delight in the LORD,
    and he will give you your heart's desires.

Commit everything you do to the LORD.
    Trust him, and he will help you.

He will make your innocence radiate like the dawn,
> and the justice of your cause will shine like the noonday
> sun.

Be still in the presence of the Lord,
> and wait patiently for him to act.
Don't worry about evil people who prosper
> or fret about their wicked schemes.[9]

"I'm Overwhelmed!"— When You Are at Your Wit's End

The feeling of being overwhelmed can hit us from many different angles. We may have a day when work issues, kids' activities, and home responsibilities pile up all at once, and we feel as though we want to scream! Overwhelming feelings may hit as difficulties pile up in a day, or they may hit us when the unexpected happens. An unplanned event or an immediate crisis can easily usher us into an overwhelmed state and send us into wondering how we are going to survive. Granted, some personalities are naturally calmer, while others become quickly frazzled; but we are all vulnerable to overwhelming feelings at times.

Such was the case in the home of Mary and Martha. When Jesus and the disciples came for a visit, the house was abuzz with activity. "Where will everyone sit?" and "How am I going to feed all these people?" were probably questions swirling around in Martha's mind, as she was the more practical-minded sister. Mary, on the other hand, chose to sit at Jesus' feet and hear his wonderful words of wisdom and truth, thinking the details could wait. Mary's attitude didn't sit so well with Martha.

Since Martha didn't have a Costco or Sam's Club in the area, feeding a crowd was a big task. Jesus knew about feeding crowds, because he had recently fed the five thousand with only a few loaves of bread and some fish.[10] Ironically, we find Martha in the kitchen feeling frazzled about a task Jesus could choose to handle in an instant.

Martha allowed her frustration to reach a peak level. In exasperation, she interrupted Jesus and pointed to Mary. "Lord, doesn't it seem unfair to you that my sister just sits here while I do all the work? Tell her to come and help me."[11] Funny how she thought Mary would be the answer to her problems, when Jesus was sitting right there. Are you as guilty as I am of pointing the finger at someone else to fix the situation, when we should be looking to Jesus and finding our peace there?

I wonder if Mary chose to sit at Jesus' feet because she was well aware of his recent feeding of the multitudes. Perhaps she chose to rest in knowing he could handle the situation if necessary. When our hearts and minds are filled with the knowledge of what God can do, we have a renewed sense of peace. Instead of blaming others or trying to accomplish everything on our own, we may need to stop and listen to the Lord. Jesus' response to Martha's exasperation offers a lesson to us as well: "My dear Martha, you are worried and upset over all these details! There is only one thing worth being concerned about. Mary has discovered it, and it will not be taken away from her."[12]

Martha has a decision to make. Will she trust God, or will she trust her own work and ability? The rest of the story is not revealed, but I sure wish it were. I wonder if Martha decided to stop her scurrying and sit down to listen to the Master. I wonder if after Jesus was finished teaching, he instructed Mary to help Martha. Of course, on the other hand, I wonder if he just chose to break bread and miraculously feed everyone himself as he had done before. Whatever happened, we do learn the importance of sitting at Jesus' feet and listening to his instructions.

When we reach a point of feeling overwhelmed and as though we can't handle the monumental task ahead of us, let's take a tip from Mary and choose to sit at Jesus' feet and hear his instruction. This is the place where we find peace. Acknowledge God for who he is, the sovereign God and Creator of all things. He is mighty to save and able to deliver you.[13] When we recognize what God has done in the past as we read his Word, our faith increases and our worry begins to diminish. Instead of putting our eyes of blame on another person, let's put our eyes of faith on Jesus. He may send someone to help, or he may instruct us as to our next steps.

"I'm Scared!"—Facing Unexpected Fears

Float with me back to a boat on the Sea of Galilee, a body of water 680 feet below sea level and surrounded by hills. The topography lends itself to violent and unexpected storms as winds blow over the land and intensify close to the sea. As evening approaches, Jesus gets in the boat and says to his disciples, "Let's cross to the other side of the lake." Shortly into the journey, one of those fierce storms comes upon them. High waves break into the boat, filling it with water.

I'm already relating to this story; how about you? It's interesting how quickly storms can hit our lives. We may be merrily rowing along on our pleasant life journeys when, without any warning, a storm changes everything and we feel as though we are sinking fast. Been there? Perhaps you have had several small storms, or maybe you have had a major storm that will mark your life forever. Whatever your storm, great or small, remember Jesus is in the boat with you.

The gospel of Mark goes on to tell us that Jesus was sleeping in the back of the boat with his head on a cushion. The desperate and frantic disciples woke him up, shouting, "Teacher, don't you even care that we are going to drown?" In the middle of your storm you may have prayed that same thing. I suppose it is hard for us to imagine that Jesus allows us to go through the storm. "Don't you care that this is happening to me? Where are you? Why are you sleeping?" we cry out to the Lord. Even though it seems like Jesus is sleeping, he does care about your situation, just as he cared for his disciples in the boat.

Jesus got up and rebuked the wind and said to the water, "Quiet down!" Suddenly the wind stopped, and there was a great calm. Jesus then had a question for the disciples: "Why are you so afraid? Do you still not have faith in me?" I believe the disciples were filled with anxiety and fear because they still didn't understand who Jesus was and what he could do. After Jesus calmed the storm, they proclaimed, "Who is this man, that even the wind and waves obey him?"[14] Jesus, the Son of God and Creator of all, was in the boat with them. They had a choice to be filled with terror or to trust the power of God. We, too, have a choice to panic or to pray when we face fearful and unexpected storms. Jesus does care, and he is in the boat with us. He may not take away the storm, but he can give us peace and calm in the midst of it.

> *We have a choice to panic or to pray when we face fearful and unexpected storms.*

In my simplistic way of seeing life, it seems to me that if Jesus is in charge of the weather, couldn't he have just made it smooth sailing the whole way? Wouldn't it have been easier on the boat and on the disciples' nerves to just skip the storm altogether and travel safely to the other side? Yet how could the disciples' faith grow unless they experienced God's miraculous power themselves? The storm allowed the disciples to see the mighty hand of God at work. They learned more about who Jesus was and what he was capable of doing through the storm, not the calm. They also learned that they could depend on him no matter what happened, for they knew he was able to handle it.

Unexpected storms will come in our lives. The question is, will we try to ride out the storm on our own in a state of panic, or will we go to Jesus first, seeking his peace and help? Jesus is in the boat with us and will never leave us. As we get to know Jesus better through studying the Bible and abiding in prayer, we begin to recognize and trust his mighty power and his ability to save us.

I like what the apostle Peter (who was one of the disciples in the boat) has to say about God's power in our lives: "By his divine power, God has given us everything we need for living a godly life. We have received all of this by coming to know him, the one who called us to himself by means of his marvelous glory and excellence. And because of his glory and excellence, he has given us great and precious promises. These are the promises that enable you to share his divine nature and escape the world's corruption caused by human desires."[15] Do you see Jesus as one who cares for you and is able to calm the storm, or do you see him as just a guy in the boat? Perhaps a guy you visit on Sunday mornings sometimes? As you get to know Jesus better and recognize who he is, your anxieties begin to subside and a precious peace takes over.

Winning the Battle in Your Brain

Did you catch the underlying theme in each of the tales about worriers who turned into warriors for God? I heard the beauty of God's loving voice telling Moses, Martha, and the disciples the same message, "I am with you." We heard it on the mountain, we saw him in the midst of Martha's busy activities, and we recognized his presence in the boat with the disciples. Now, my friend, I encourage you to hear his voice whispering in your ear, "I am with you. Trust me. Abide with me." It is time to lay down our fears at his feet. Peter reminds us, "Give all your worries and cares to God, for he cares about you."[16] I suppose he learned that firsthand!

Pride says, "I can handle this myself." Fear says, "I can't handle this at all." Humility says, "My trust is in the Lord." If we are to thrive, not simply survive, we must move to a place of faith, and not fear. I want to challenge you to cast your cares on him as a daily routine in your life, just like brushing your teeth or combing your hair. To tell you truthfully, although I've had a daily prayer time for quite a while, I had never set aside a time to give my fears over to God. It was almost like I didn't want to acknowledge them, so I just let my worries and anxieties float around in my brain undisturbed. I didn't do anything to them, but they sure did a number of me! My fears dominated my thoughts and my actions.

Every morning, I take a long walk. It's my time to pray and devote the day to God. I always need to stretch before I walk; and so now while I stretch, I make a point of recognizing my fears and giving them over to God. Just as stretching and working out is a part of my daily routine, so casting my cares on him and walking in prayer should be a daily practice as well. Acknowledging my worries and asking God to give me his peace has been a good process for me personally. When I deliberately look at my anxieties and give them over to the Lord, he provides a calm that can only come from him.

> *I am amazed at how many little worries I have welcomed and allowed to dwell in my mind over the years.*

Stop a moment and think about the worries, cares, and fears you have allowed to hang out in your skull. Is there a daily time when you can deliberately give those cares to God? Ask the Lord to help you see some of these manipulative and stealth anxieties, and then ask God to take those fears away and replace them with peace. Personally, I am amazed at how many little worries I have welcomed and allowed to dwell in my mind over the years; yet with God's help, they have dwindled.

We must recognize these anxieties for what they are: unwanted enemies. They undermine our trust in God and lead us away from growing in faith. Worrying makes us a prisoner of war, locked behind the bars of our own fears and doubts. What if Moses had allowed his fears to take over his mind and he never went to Pharaoh? What if the disciples tried to handle the storm on their own and never woke Jesus? What if Martha continued to feed her feelings of being overwhelmed, keeping it all bottled up inside? We can just imagine what kind of explosion would have taken place at her house, can't we, girls?

When we recognize this enemy called worry and replace it with seeking God, a peace begins to fill our souls. We begin to think and speak and act differently. We begin to thrive. When our eyes are on God, we begin to step out in faith and follow what God is calling us to do, rather than being caged in with worry and fear. The Supreme Commander of the heavenly armies wants us to give him our cares and concerns. We may not know what the outcome will be, but we do know he will be with us through the battles ahead.

His presence is our peace. Just the fact of knowing God is with us begins to settle our anxious feelings. Since worries like to pop back into our thinking, we must routinely give them to him. As I mentioned earlier, I cast my fears on God during my daily stretching routine. How will you fit your daily casting into a smooth routine? Maybe while you brush your teeth or wash the dishes or do the laundry. Make it a daily action to acknowledge your fears and ask God to replace them with his peace.

Who can say it better than the apostle Paul?

> Don't worry about anything; instead, pray about everything. Tell God what you need, and thank him for all he has done. Then you will experience God's peace, which exceeds anything we can understand. His peace will guard your hearts and minds as you live in Christ Jesus.

And now, dear brothers and sisters, one final thing. Fix your thoughts on what is true, and honorable, and right, and pure, and lovely, and admirable. Think about things that are excellent and worthy of praise.[17]

Paul gave the early Christians basic training in worry warfare. As they faced unknown obstacles and the potential of persecution, Paul wanted to help them live in peace instead of constant anxiety. He encouraged them to allow their faith to shine brilliantly in the form of a peace that passes all understanding. Just as an army is identified by its uniforms, so we as Christians can be identified by the peace and joy that is evident in our lives—even lives that have taken a path different from what we'd hoped for. What do people see when they look at you and me? Do they see a woman of worry, or do they see a woman walking in trust? Scripture tell us that those who look to him are radiant. With eyes of faith on the Lord, we can beam with a radiance of confident trust.

STEPPING FORWARD

 ### POINTS

- Unexpected challenges are the incubator for negative worry or positive change.
- A healthy concern can be the catalyst to help us to take positive steps forward.
- Worry-free living should not be an excuse for irresponsibility.
- When you feel inadequate, overwhelmed, or afraid, remember God is with you and will equip you.
- Take time to step aside from your busyness and consult the Lord.

- Recognize that God cares for you and wants you to trust him.
- Worry is like an enemy that keeps us in prison and prevents us from stepping out in faith.
- Change the way you think by daily giving your cares to God and replacing them with thoughts of hope and faith.

 ### PASSAGE: PSALM 46:1–11

God is our refuge and strength,
    always ready to help in times of trouble.
So we will not fear when earthquakes come
    and the mountains crumble into the sea.
Let the oceans roar and foam.
    Let the mountains tremble as the waters surge!

A river brings joy to the city of our God,
    the sacred home of the Most High.
God dwells in that city; it cannot be destroyed.
    From the very break of day, God will protect it.
The nations are in chaos,
    and their kingdoms crumble!
God's voice thunders,
    and the earth melts!
The LORD of Heaven's Armies is here among us;
    the God of Israel is our fortress.

Come, see the glorious works of the LORD:
    See how he brings destruction upon the world.
He causes wars to end throughout the earth.
    He breaks the bow and snaps the spear;
    he burns the shields with fire.

"Be still, and know that I am God!
  I will be honored by every nation.
  I will be honored throughout the world."

The LORD of Heaven's Armies is here among us;
  the God of Israel is our fortress.

PRAYER

Great and glorious God, you are able to do all things. You know all things, and you are everywhere. I praise you as the Creator of the universe and the lover of my soul. I want to know you more. I want to abide with you and trust you. It is easy for me to worry, especially when I don't know how things will turn out. Oh Lord, help me to seek you first and to hear your voice saying, *Do not be afraid. I am with you, my dear child.* Show me and guide me where to walk in faith and not be caged in by my fears. In Jesus' name, amen.

PLAN

Begin a daily routine of casting your cares upon the Lord. It may be while you are washing the dishes or brushing your teeth or driving to work. Choose a time and a place and write it here: _____

_____

It takes twenty-one days to form a habit, so discipline yourself for twenty-one days to carry out this routine. Mark it off on your calendar, so you can chart your progress.

Dear friend, as you begin this new routine of casting your cares on the Lord, I encourage you to spend time praising God each day for who he is and what he can do. As you praise and acknowledge him as a sovereign and powerful God, you will find your trust in him increasing while your worries and fears decrease.

O love of God, how strong and true!
Eternal, and yet ever new;
Uncomprehended and unbought,
Beyond all knowledge and all thought.

Horatius Bonar

4

How Can I Trust a God Who Allows Pain and Suffering?

Deepening Your Faith in the Lover of Your Soul

"My thoughts are nothing like your thoughts," says the LORD.
"And my ways are far beyond anything you could imagine.
For just as the heavens are higher than the earth,
so my ways are higher than your ways
And my thoughts higher than your thoughts."

Isaiah 55:8–9

Edie (pronounced E-dee) met Greg when they were both students at the University of Missouri. They soon married, and their precious daughter, Amanda, was born five years later. Greg was the love of Edie's life. After fifteen years of a healthy and strong marriage, Greg was diagnosed with a rare form of aggressive cancer. Four months later, Edie was planning his funeral. She never pictured herself as a single mother, but it became her new identity at the young age of thirty-seven. Edie had strength and support from family and friends, but most important, she was buoyed by God's care. She grieved, but she also knew God would take care of her. Although she couldn't understand why God allowed this to happen, Edie sensed God's presence in her life.

Out of necessity, Edie needed to create some income, so her friends encouraged her to take a few classes in faux finishing and other painting techniques. Edie's friends knew that she had a decorator's eye for color and texture, so they pushed her to explore and enrich her talents in order to embark on a new business adventure. And she did! Her work took off as people recognized her talent and hired her to redo the walls of their homes. It became a full-time job.

Edie was reluctant to begin dating, yet her marriage to Greg had been so fulfilling that she longed for that kind of happiness again. She also wanted a father figure for Amanda. One source of encouragement and joy for Edie was her tennis team. She was and still is an avid tennis player. Not long after Greg's death, her tennis team decided to switch locations and join a new club. Edie went right along with them. At the same time, by God's divine plan, a tennis coach named Mark decided to take a temporary job at that very club.

Slowly and dearly, Mark and Edie fell in love. Mark's family not only embraced Edie, but they loved and embraced Amanda as well. Mark didn't have any children, so Amanda was their first grandchild. When Edie and Mark married, Amanda received an additional set of adoring grandparents as a bonus. Amanda blessed Mark as much as Mark blessed her. Mark will even tell you that he had been a bit self-centered, living to please himself, yet his new family had a powerful effect on him and served as a stabilizing factor and a lesson in selflessness.

As God began working in Mark's heart, Mark realized he wanted to give back to society and do something significant for others. He called his grandfather, who served on the board for Providence House Ministries, based in Denver, Colorado. Providence House offers life-changing, Christ-centered help for homeless, abused, and formerly incarcerated women and their children. Their objective is to help women get back on their feet again in every aspect of life. They have numerous houses in Denver, but Dallas (where Mark and Edie live) didn't have a Providence House. Mark took on the huge task of bringing Providence House Ministries to Dallas. Miracle upon miracle occurred, and God supplied abundantly for the ministry to begin. At the time of this writing, there are two Providence Houses in the Dallas area, and you can expect more in the future!

Reflecting back on Greg's death, Edie says she may never fully understand why God would allow her vibrant, dear husband (and Amanda's father) to die at such an early age, but she has been able to experience God's provision and see his blessing. Edie knows Greg is with the Lord, and she sees the amazing hand of God in this new and exciting chapter in her life. Exploring her creative side, finding a wonderful new extended family, and inspiring a man to start an amazing ministry are some of the blessings Edie can see this side of the tragedy. Most important, Edie says she was able to demonstrate resiliency for her daughter as she moved forward in faith, trusting God would take care of them.

Maybe you are wondering why God would allow someone to die in the prime of life. Or perhaps you are asking, "Why doesn't God answer my prayers?" "Why was I born this way?" "Why didn't God rescue me out of my misery?" The problem of pain and suffering is an age-old philosophical question. If God is a good, loving, and sovereign God, then why does he allow evil and hurt in the world? We somehow think that if we knew why we were suffering, we could handle it better. Does it feel that way to you? We may not have the luxury of knowing the answers to why we suffer this side of heaven, yet as strange as it may sound, sometimes we can see a benefit to pain.

Christian apologist and author Norman Geisler elaborates:

Even in our finiteness, it is possible for humans to discover some good purposes for pain—such as warning us of greater evil (an infant need only touch a hot stove once to learn not to do it again), and to keep us from self-destruction (our built-in nerve endings detect pain so we won't, for example, continue to hold a hot pan in our hands). If finite humans can discover some good purposes for evil, then surely an infinitely wise God has a good purpose for all suffering. We may not understand that purpose in the temporal 'now,' but it nonetheless exists. Our inability to discern why bad things sometimes happen to us does not disprove God's benevolence; it merely exposes our ignorance.[1]

In this chapter, we not only want to grow in our understanding and trust of God, but we also want to begin to make some sense of suffering.

Can God Be Trusted?

In the Old Testament, we read about a man named Job who found himself struggling to understand why. His vibrant, fruitful world came to a crashing halt when God allowed him to suffer the loss of his possessions, his children, and his health. He couldn't understand why this would happen to him as he had been a noble and upright man. Job's not-so-helpful friends tried to give him answers, leaning on what they thought was a logical premise. They thought suffering was simply a result of sin. God eventually let them know they did not speak accurately about him.

> *"I had only heard about you before, but now I have seen you with my own eyes."—Job 42:5*

God lovingly responded to Job's unsettled questions of the heart. Instead of explaining the reasons Job suffered, God kindly directed Job back to an authentic trust in a God he could not understand. God asked Job, "Where were you when I laid the foundations of the earth? Tell me, if you know so much."[2] God led Job to a deeper understanding of his almighty power and omniscience. Job finally declared to God, "I know that you can do anything, and no one can stop you. You asked, 'Who is this that questions my wisdom with such ignorance?' It is I—and I was talking about things I knew nothing about, things far too wonderful for me. . . . I had only heard about you before, but now I have seen you with my own eyes."[3]

We must ask ourselves, are we willing to trust God even though we don't understand his ways? It's hard, I know. Direct answers would be much nicer. How do we grow to the point of trust? How can we rest in the arms of a loving God when we can't understand why he allows certain difficulties? Certainly we cannot know all the answers, but as we draw close to God, we begin to get to know who he is and what he is about. We develop a trust in the God who loves us. In this passage about Job, notice he said he had heard about God, but now he has seen him with his eyes. Job moved from a point of knowing about God to a place of truly experiencing him.

Job was able to put his trust in a God he knew, not just in one he had heard about. The same is true with us. We can find people's opinions about God from books, commentaries, editorials, and even sermons on Sundays, but we must get to know him for ourselves. A search for the truth about God will lead us to an understanding of his trustworthiness. It's one thing to know about God in a distant sort of way; it is another thing to experience him up close and personal. As we get to know him, our hearts are drawn into a love relationship with him.

Saint Bernard of Clairvaux said, "If we begin to worship and come to God again and again by meditating, by reading, by prayer, and by obedience, little by little God becomes known to us through experience. We enter into a sweet familiarity with God, and by tasting how sweet the Lord is we pass into . . . loving God, not for our own sake, but for Himself."[4] We can fall into the arms of a God whom we know and love, but it is difficult to trust someone we do not know personally.

As Job learned, we cannot understand all of God's ways, but there are certain qualities we can know about him. Where do we begin our journey of knowing him? The Bible gives us glimpses of the High King of heaven and his marvelous attributes. Here are a few of the numerous qualities we learn about God as we see them revealed in the Bible. I have provided just one biblical reference for each attribute, although there are numerous others.

He is:

Almighty (Genesis 17:1)
Everlasting (Genesis 21:33)
All-Powerful (2 Chronicles 20:6)
Abundant in Strength (Psalm 147:5)
Abounding in Love (Psalm 103:8)
Sovereign (Deuteronomy 3:24)
Merciful (Psalm 62:12)
Trustworthy (2 Samuel 22:3)
Our Keeper (Psalm 121:7–8)
Our Provider (Matthew 6:26)
Our Good Shepherd (John 10:11)
Able—nothing is too difficult for him (Genesis 18:14)

I want to get to know a God like this, don't you? Certainly if God is who the Bible says he is, then he is worthy of our respect, obedience, and, yes, trust. Consider where you are with God right now in your life. What do you believe about him? We don't want to make assumptions about God; rather, we want to explore who he claims to be. As we get to know the God of the Bible, we begin to recognize his abiding love for us. He is worthy of our trust. I encourage you to continue your journey of engagement with God.

Based on what I have learned from the Bible, here's what I personally believe about God: I believe he is a loving, compassionate, merciful God. I believe he sent his Son, Jesus, to die on the cross as payment for our sins. I believe Jesus rose again, offering us the promise of eternal life in heaven one day with him. I believe he has provided his Spirit to live in our lives to help us, comfort us, and guide us in truth. I believe he will never leave us. I believe he is a sovereign God who can do all things, knows all things, and sees all things.

What do you believe? Take a moment to write out your statement of belief. Consider why you believe what you believe. Don't just let what you see on television or hear from friends determine your own personal belief system. If you believe there is a God, then he rightfully deserves to be investigated. Get to know him. Search the Bible and see what it has to say about him. If we ultimately want to be able to trust him, we need to get to know who he is. How can you trust someone you don't know?

How can you trust someone you don't know?

John Calvin said, "Our inklings of the realities of God will be vague and smudged until we learn from Scripture to think correctly about the realities of which we are already aware." He added, "Unless God's Word illumine the way, the whole life of men is wrapped in darkness and mist, so that they cannot but miserably stray."[5] We don't want to wander aimlessly in our misery or stumble in the dark without hope, simply because we haven't taken the time to get to know the God of the Bible. He is worthy of our trust and welcomes us into a loving relationship with him.

Making Sense of Misery

From our perspective, things can look bleak and dismal, but does that mean that all hope is gone or that God doesn't love us? No, it simply means we don't have an eternal understanding of what is going on. The apostle Paul knew what it was like to have setbacks and challenges and to be confined. He also recognized he didn't have all the answers for his sufferings, but he knew they were a part of a greater purpose. Here's how he described his challenges in his ministry:

> We have this treasure in jars of clay to show that this all-surpassing power is from God and not from us. We are hard pressed on every side, but not crushed; perplexed, but not in despair; persecuted, but not abandoned; struck down, but not destroyed. We always carry around in our body the death of Jesus, so that the life of Jesus may also be revealed in our body. For we who are alive are always being given over to death for Jesus' sake, so that his life may be revealed in our mortal body. So then, death is at work in us, but life is at work in you. . . .
>
> Therefore we do not lose heart. Though outwardly we are wasting away, yet inwardly we are being renewed day by day. For our light and momentary troubles are achieving for us an eternal glory that far outweighs them all. So we fix our eyes not on what is seen, but on what is unseen. For what is seen is temporary, but what is unseen is eternal.[6]

According to Paul, there is a reason for our suffering. Our current troubles achieve for us an eternal glory that far outweighs the momentary suffering here on earth. So there is something bigger going on here, an eternal plan. It involves much more than our own personal world and our present difficult lives. Consider the possible benefits (yes, benefits) of our challenges and sufferings. Now, I offer these to you gently, recognizing your pain may be heavy and your heart may be tender. If you are in the midst of severe hurt and cannot see hope

> *Consider the possible benefits (yes, benefits) of our challenges and sufferings.*

yet, this section may be too difficult to read right now. Although it is truth, you may need to reflect on this truth after you have worked through some of the initial pain. So if you are in the midst of severe grief, I suggest you skip this section for right now and then come back to it a little later when your wound or pain is not quite as raw.

For those who are ready to hear, the Bible gives us several clues as to the benefits of our challenges. I'm certainly not trying to give simple answers to your grief; I am presenting some of the possibilities for good that can emerge out of challenges we face.

First, *trials offer us a chance to grow.* Our character is built and we become a stronger person through the challenges in life. In the book of James, we find words of encouragement toward the difficulties we face: "Dear brothers and sisters, when troubles come your way, consider it an opportunity for great joy. For you know that when your faith is tested, your endurance has a chance to grow. So let it grow, for when your endurance is fully developed, you will be perfect and complete, needing nothing."[7]

Second, *trials offer us an opportunity to empathize with and encourage others.* Paul gave hope to the persecuted believers by saying, "God is our merciful Father and the source of all comfort. He comforts us in all our troubles so that we can comfort others. When they are troubled, we will be able to give them the same comfort God has given us. For the more we suffer for Christ, the more God will shower us with his comfort through Christ. Even when we are weighed down with troubles, it is for your comfort and salvation! For when we ourselves are comforted, we will certainly comfort you. Then you can patiently endure the same things we suffer."[8]

Third, *trials remind us of our need for God's care and help.* Instead of arrogantly thinking we can live life by ourselves, trials bring us back to placing our trust in God and seeking his will for our lives. Listen to David's words:

Though the LORD is great, he cares for the humble,
    but he keeps his distance from the proud.

Though I am surrounded by troubles,
    you will protect me from the anger of my enemies.
You reach out your hand,
    and the power of your right hand saves me.
The LORD will work out his plans for my life—
    for your faithful love, O LORD, endures forever.
    Don't abandon me, for you made me.[9]

Fourth, *trials often lead us back to our loving God.* Instead of allowing us to go astray, God at times uses trials in our lives to draw us lovingly back to himself. Once again in the Psalms, we read:

The LORD is good and does what is right;
he shows the proper path to those who go astray.
He leads the humble in doing right,
teaching them his way.[10]

Fifth, *trials are sometimes God's way of disciplining his children.* As a loving parent teaches, trains, and disciplines his children, so the Lord does the same for those he loves. Certainly not all challenges in our lives fall into the category of discipline from the Lord, but the Bible tells us there are times when the Lord uses hardships to discipline us. The writer of Hebrews said:

Endure hardship as discipline; God is treating you as sons. For what son is not disciplined by his father? If you are not disciplined (and everyone undergoes discipline), then you are illegitimate children and not true sons. Moreover, we have all had human fathers who disciplined us and we respected them for it. How much more should we submit to the Father of our spirits and live! Our fathers disciplined us for a little while as they thought best; but God disciplines us for our good, that we may share in his holiness. No discipline seems pleasant at the time, but painful. Later on, however, it produces a harvest of righteousness and peace for those who have been trained by it.[11]

Sixth, *trials allow us, in a small way, to share in the sufferings of Christ.* The apostle Peter reminded the early Christians, "Dear friends, don't be surprised at the fiery trials you are going through, as if something strange were happening to you. Instead, be very glad—for these trials make you partners with Christ in his suffering, so that you will have the wonderful joy of seeing his glory when it is revealed to all the world."[12]

Certainly this is not an exhaustive list of all the reasons you might go through trials. And I don't want to be like Job's friends, who seemed to think they knew exactly why Job was suffering. I simply want to point out that the Bible gives us some insight into how we can make some sense out of trials and why

> *Trials point us to an opportunity to trust him and watch him open up new doors.*

God uses them sometimes in our lives. As we saw in Edie's story, God may use a difficult experience to lead us down a fresh and different path in life. Trials certainly don't indicate that God has left us or forgotten us; rather, they point us to an opportunity to trust him and watch him open up new doors.

Divine Grace?

Dr. Paul Lanier was a successful doctor, hunter, and pilot. He was a healthy and vibrant man until he began to experience some curious physical symptoms. As a doctor, he was well aware of the terrible suffering those with ALS (Lou Gehrig's disease) experience, so you can imagine his devastation when, at age thirty-seven, he received the diagnosis that he himself had the disease. Yet instead of living in anger toward God, Dr. Lanier began to explore what God wanted to teach him through his suffering. Dr. Lanier began to write out his thoughts as he wrestled with suffering and loss.

As the disease progressed, he eventually lost the use of his arms. Although bound to a wheelchair, his neck and legs had slight movement. Dr. Lanier was able to continue typing with the use of a laser beam strapped to his head. Painstakingly he pointed to a letter on his computer screen and clicked the mouse that was strapped to his knees (thank goodness for technology!). Pointing and clicking, he lovingly poured out the lessons God taught him through the seat of suffering.

As a former pilot, Dr. Lanier had learned all about registering his flight plan with the aviation towers, yet his life message became a change in flight plan. With the help of his friend Dave Turtletaub, he wrote a book by that title. *A Change in the Flight Plan* is a compilation of Dr. Lanier's thoughts and meditations on God's truth and lessons he has learned about suffering. Concerning the grace of suffering he wrote, "Anything that God permits to happen to us in this life, whether good or bad, that better prepares us to meet Him as we approach the threshold of eternity, can only be interpreted as grace on His part."[13]

Take time to ponder Dr. Lanier's thought about the grace of suffering. Could it be that the disappointments or suffering in life are actually a form of God's loving grace? If it were simply me telling you this truth while I sit here nicely at my computer, writing, you may question the veracity of this statement. But when you read it from Dr. Lanier's point of view, written from a wheelchair while suffering one of the most dreaded diseases of mankind, your eyes are opened to a new reality of pain.

Charles Spurgeon, in his wonderful devotional called *Morning and Evening Daily Readings*, addresses the purpose for pain in this same vein. He, too, sees trials through the lens of divine grace. Here we see Spurgeon's perspective as he expounded on a passage from Job:

"Shew me wherefore thou contendest with me." Job 10:2

Perhaps, O tried soul, the Lord is doing this to develop thy graces. There are some of thy graces which would never be discovered if it were not for thy trials. Dost thou not know that thy faith never looks so grand in summer weather as it does in winter? Love is too often like a glow-worm, showing but little light except it be in the midst of surrounding darkness. Hope itself is like a star—not to be seen in the sunshine of prosperity, and only to be discovered in the night of adversity. Afflictions are often the black foils in which God doth set the jewels of his children's graces, to make them shine the better. It was but a little while ago that on thy knees thou wast saying, "Lord, I fear I have no faith: let me know that I have faith." Was not this really, though perhaps unconsciously, praying for trials?—for how canst thou know that thou hast faith until thy faith is exercised? Depend upon it, God often sends us trials that our graces may be discovered, and that we may be certified of their existence. Besides, it is not merely discovery, real growth in grace is the result of sanctified trials. God often takes away our comforts and our privileges in order to make us better Christians. He trains his soldiers, not in tents of ease and luxury, but by turning them out and using them to forced marches and hard service. He makes them ford through streams, and swim through rivers, and climb mountains, and walk many a long mile with heavy knapsacks of sorrow on their backs. Well,

Christian, may not this account for the troubles through which thou art passing? Is not the Lord bringing out your graces, and making them grow? Is not this the reason why he is contending with you?

Trials make the promise sweet;
Trials give new life to prayer,
Trials bring me to His feet,
Lay me low, and keep me there.[14]

The Lover of Our Souls

Spurgeon's words paint a wider and broader picture of God's love and care for us. Our eyes are opened to God's desire to encourage our growth and strength. He genuinely cares about our development in grace and knows that if we stay in the luxury of comfort, no growth will take place. Yes, the God of all creation loves us so much that he won't allow us to stay stagnant.

Here's a personal analogy. Just a few days ago, I went to the veterinarian to pick up some medication for my English mastiff. Whenever I go to the vet, I see a wide variety of animals with all degrees of ailments and injuries. As I was on my way out of the vet building, another woman was leaving with her precious yet very unhappy beagle. The beagle's unhappiness was due to the fact he was being forced to wear a lampshade around his neck. It wasn't really a lampshade; it was one of those cone collars that prevents a dog from chewing on his stitches. Surely there has got to be a better way!

This bumbling beagle was bumping into everything (doors, cabinets, people) and whining with every hit. It was a sad picture. The owner looked at me and said, "Can you believe he is going to have to wear this for a week?"

Poor thing! It looked to me like it was going to be torture for him just to make it through the day, much less a week! The owner then said, "If he only knew it was there to help him get better. I wish I could tell him the plastic guard is for his best interest, and I'm doing this to him because I love him." I promise you she did not know I was writing this chapter!

There are a few life lessons we can learn from our little furry friend. The owner put the lampshade on the dog to help him experience the greatest amount of healing and benefit. But from the dog's perspective, wearing the cone collar most likely seemed cruel. He couldn't understand why she would allow him to suffer in such a way, yet because the owner loved the dog, she wanted the best for him.

> *"If he only knew it was there to help him get better and that I'm doing this to him because I love him."*

The beagle had some choices as to how he would respond to the cone collar. He could have struggled with it, continually trying to pull it off. He could have barked and barked until the neighbors called the police. Or he could have adjusted to the cone collar and trusted the owner's love for him. Certainly trusting the owner would be the most difficult thing to do, but it would also be the most pleasant route for him.

Are you following me here? Happily, we don't have to wear lampshades around our necks, but we do have to experience situations that are uncomfortable and unexpected. The more we know the Master and trust his love for us, the more peace and calm we can experience in our journeys. God is the lover of our souls, and because he loves us, he does not simply give us every little thing we want. He sees our souls in light of eternity. He does not give us quick fixes for the here and now but prepares us for his kingdom.

Let us grasp the glorious picture here. As believers in Christ, we are part of God's family. He has lovingly adopted us and allowed us to be partakers of his grace. We can rejoice in this wonderful privilege in which we stand. We can choose to see life's rough spots as cruelty from our Master, or we can trust God's loving hand and learn and grow from these situations. We can actually come to the point (I know this may be difficult for you to believe) of rejoicing about the rough spots. Read what the apostle Paul had to say to the Romans:

> Since we have been made right in God's sight by faith, we have peace with God because of what Jesus Christ our Lord has done for us. Because of our faith, Christ has brought us into this place of undeserved privilege where we now stand, and we confidently and joyfully look forward to sharing God's glory.
>
> We can rejoice, too, when we run into problems and trials, for we know that they help us develop endurance. And endurance develops strength of character, and character strengthens our confident hope of salvation. And this hope will not lead to disappointment. For we know how dearly God loves us, because he has given us the Holy Spirit to fill our hearts with his love.[15]

Isn't that beautiful? "For we know how dearly God loves us." I hope those words sink into your spirit and sing to your soul. Why are we able to rejoice when problems come our way? Because we know how dearly God loves us and we know problems can help us grow. My friend, are you convinced that God loves you? Often we feel unlovable because of shortcomings, mistakes, and sins, yet God knows each of us through and through. That's why he sent Christ, so we may be forgiven and walk in fellowship with him. Out of his love for us, he redeemed us.

Enjoy God's love. As we get to know the God of the Bible

better, we begin to see a God who deeply cares for his people. His love letters to us are unmistakably clear. He is compassionate and gracious, slow to anger and abounding in love.[16] Oh the joy of growing in a deeper love relationship with him! Though your life has not turned out as you'd hoped and planned, with God's help you can find new hope and purpose as you thrive and grow ever deeper in love with God. Listen to his tender voice right now whispering in your ear, *I am with you. Trust me. I love you.*

STEPPING FORWARD

POINTS

- What we believe about God determines whether we will trust him.
- Base your belief about God on the Bible, not on hearsay or other people's opinions.
- The Bible tells us that God is sovereign, almighty, all-knowing, and abounding in love.
- As we grow to know God, we grow to love him and trust him.
- Trials and troubles serve a greater purpose in our lives, often beyond what we can see right now.
- God is the lover of our souls. We may not understand why he allows certain situations in our lives, but we can trust his love and his eternal purposes.

PASSAGE: PSALM 103:1–13

Let all that I am praise the LORD;
    with my whole heart, I will praise his holy name.
Let all that I am praise the LORD;
    may I never forget the good things he does for me.

He forgives all my sins
    and heals all my diseases.
He redeems me from death
    and crowns me with love and tender mercies.
He fills my life with good things.
    My youth is renewed like the eagle's!

The LORD gives righteousness
    and justice to all who are treated unfairly.

He revealed his character to Moses
    and his deeds to the people of Israel.
The LORD is compassionate and merciful,
    slow to get angry and filled with unfailing love.
He will not constantly accuse us,
    nor remain angry forever.
He does not punish us for all our sins;
    he does not deal harshly with us, as we deserve.
For his unfailing love toward those who fear him
    is as great as the height of the heavens above the
    earth.
He has removed our sins as far from us
    as the east is from the west.
The LORD is like a father to his children,
    tender and compassionate to those who fear him.

 PRAYER

Sovereign God, marvelous heavenly Father, I praise you for your compassion and love toward me. Thank you for your comfort and care through my difficulties. Thank you for hearing my prayer. Thank you for being with me right now. Forgive me when I have ignored you. Draw me close to you, and help me to know your love in a very real way. Help me to reflect that love in my relationships with others. In Jesus' name, amen.

PLAN

Set a time to meet with God every morning, even if it is a short time. This is an opportunity for you to be still and know him. Begin your time with praising God for who he is (use the passage above from Psalm 103 to help you consider some of his attributes). Confess your sins. Take time to thank God for his provisions in your life right now. Most important, thank him for sending his Son to offer forgiveness for our sins. Give God your fears and worries. As you meet with him, you will grow to love him and trust him more and more. You will also begin to experience his abiding love for you in a very real way.

Write out a personal statement of belief based on what you have learned about God in the Bible.

PART TWO

Embrace the Unexpected

*When one door of happiness closes, another opens;
but often we look so long at the closed door that we do not see
the one which has been opened for us.*

Helen Keller

*All glory to God, who is able,
through his mighty power at work within us,
to accomplish infinitely more than we might ask or think.*

Ephesians 3:20

For broken dreams the cure is,
dream again and deeper . . .

C. S. Lewis

5

The Beauty of Plan B

Finding Fresh Possibilities in New Dreams

*In his kindness God called you to share in his eternal glory
by means of Christ Jesus. So after you have suffered a little while,
he will restore, support, and strengthen you, and he will place you
on a firm foundation. All power to him forever! Amen.*

1 Peter 5:10–11

One of Kathleen's greatest joys in life is to encourage women to dream big. You would think someone with an upbeat perspective like hers would be living the life she always dreamed of. Not exactly. I recently had the opportunity to hear Kathleen speak, and I was absolutely moved by her story. She began telling the audience about a relationship that broke her heart. Here's how she put it:

I will never forget the night when I received the phone call from a man that I thought I would possibly some day marry. There were no easy words for him except, "I don't think I can see you anymore." All the playing hard to get, all the things you're told to do to help win a man left me when the tears started rolling down my face and I couldn't talk. I felt like I couldn't breathe. I mumbled a few words, hung up the phone, fell down on the couch, and cried it seemed all night long.

The thought of turning forty and not being married overwhelmed me. Why, Lord? As a little girl all I ever dreamed of doing was to grow up and get married. Isn't that what all young girls dream of doing? For days I just wanted to stay in bed. I reached a point that I knew I had to make a choice; was I going to be bitter or make the best of my life? I was faced with throwing away everything I believed in, or clinging to all the truths I had studied and learned and walk in them for one more day. Broken hearts take time to heal, and it was a daily process. I had nothing the world says makes you happy—the husband, the house, or the children.

The days passed, and gradually the biblical truths I had studied over the years began to give me hope again. The underlying theme for my existence came down to my faith. God never said that life would be easy, but He did say, "For I know the plans I have for you, plans to prosper you and not to harm you, plans to give you hope and a future" (Jeremiah 29:11 NIV). I held on to this truth.

Broken dreams . . . we all have them. But Jesus intends for me to have a life of joy despite my circumstances, a life of peace despite the storms, and a life that is complete . . . though single.

Sometimes our hearts are so set on plan A that we miss the beauty and the potential in plan B. Though God may not purpose pain and suffering for our lives, a turn of events comes as no surprise to God. And if we will trust in him, he *will* bring good out of pain. Seeing the beauty in our plan B is a matter of changing our focus and recognizing that God has a plan that far exceeds our vision. When our lives change or simply don't go the way we thought they would, we can choose to enjoy the detour or live in frustration. Now just to reiterate, I'm not saying that we ought to avoid grieving over the loss of our dreams and plans. It is healthy to recognize the loss of the dream and grieve it, but then we must look ahead to what God has in front of us.

> *When our dreams change, the words new and different replace the words old and comfortable.*

No matter what the loss, hope can always be found. When our dreams change, the words *new* and *different* replace the words *old* and *comfortable*. Have you ever noticed that when you buy a product labeled *new*, you typically see the word *improved* as well? I've never seen a bottle labeled "new and worse." New can often be better. That's what this chapter is all about—the "new and improved" life you now live! It is through the disappointments in life that we can choose to grow and change for the better.

There is a beauty to be found in plan B, but we may need to open our eyes a bit wider and change our focus in order to find the treasure. In this chapter, I will give you the tools to help you uncover the treasure and find the joy in your new journey. We will use the first four letters of the alphabet to help you remember the tools. I guess you could call it the ABCDs of seeing the treasure in the turn your life has taken.

A. Assess the Possibilities God has Provided

You've grieved your loss, you've set your worries aside, and you've come to a point of accepting your new reality; now it is time to assess the possibilities in your life. Consider the doors which can be opened in front of you, and, yes, there are wonderful doors filled with opportunities in front of you. You may not have wanted to look at them. You may have felt overwhelmed and didn't know how to look for them, but now it's time to explore the beauty in the life that lies ahead of you.

Let's take a deliberate look at your possibilities. As we begin this adventure in exploring the potential new plans for your life, I want to encourage you to begin by approaching God and seeking his wisdom and help. The writer of Hebrews encourages us to approach the throne of grace because we have a high priest, Jesus, who understands what we are going through. "For we do not have a high priest who is unable to sympathize with our weaknesses, but we have one who has been tempted in every way, just as we are—yet was without sin. Let us then approach the throne of grace with confidence, so that we may receive mercy and find grace to help us in our time of need." (verses 4:15–16)[1]

As you prayerfully assess the possibilities in your life, I want to encourage you to not only go to God for guidance, help, and wisdom, but I also want to encourage you to find a trusted friend or family member to help you look objectively at your opportunities. Carefully and honestly answer the following questions on your own, then share your answers with someone who will give you wise and godly counsel as you proceed.

What are the good things about my life right now?

What positive actions can I take without neglecting my commitments?

What gifts and talents has God given me?

How could I use at least one of these gifts or talents in a new and fresh way?

What opportunities has God placed in my life right now? They may not be fun or glamorous, but I'll write down all opportunities God has provided.

If I were going to dream big, what would I love to do with the life God has given me?

What resources or knowledge do I have available to accomplish these dreams?

What resources or knowledge do I need to obtain in order to move forward?

Who are the people God has placed in my life whom I can bless and who may be a blessing to me as well?

As you take an intentional look at the possibilities in your life perhaps you will see a glimmer of hope. The potential for new dreams exists, yet so often the frustrations and disappointments cloud our view, and we fail to recognize the open door to new dreams. We simply survive when we choose to ignore the opportunities, but we begin to thrive when we look with anticipation at what God can do. Assessing the possibilities God has placed in our lives eventually leads us to a place of experiencing a renewed joy and strength.

B. Believe He Is Able to Bring a Wonderful New Plan

God brings beauty from ashes, calm from chaos, and redemption when all seems lost. My friend, do not lose hope. You may not be able to see the light at the end of the tunnel right now. You may not be able to dream or fathom how anything good could come from your heartache. You may not know what to do next, but I want to be a voice of encouragement to you with one simple word—*believe*. Scottish theologian Marcus Dods said, "We are not to think that, where we see no possibility, God sees none."[2]

> *God brings beauty from ashes, calm from chaos, and redemption when all seems lost.*

If you struggle with believing that God can bring something good from your rubble, approach God and ask him to help you believe. You won't be the first one to do that. We read in the gospel of Mark that a certain man brought his ailing son to Jesus, seeking healing and help. He said, "Have mercy on us and help us, if you can." Jesus responded, "What do you mean, 'If I can?' Anything is possible if a person believes." The father instantly cried out, "I do believe, but help me overcome my unbelief!"[3]

We can offer a similar request: "Lord, I want to believe, but

I'm not quite there yet; help me believe you have something better in store. Open my eyes to the beauty of your plan." As you pray that prayer, you are opening your heart to believing God.

Believing God doesn't mean you can see the answer in sight. In fact, believing God means that although you don't see the answer, you still have faith. Take a look at the description of faith found in Hebrews: "Now faith is being sure of what we hope for and certain of what we do not see."[4] Faith isn't built on what we can clearly see, but rather on the hope of what we cannot yet see. We don't need faith if we can see the complete picture of plan B in sight, but our faith grows like a weed when we place our trust in God and believe he will care for us when we can't yet see the outcome.

Belief takes our eyes off our old and fading dreams and puts them on the God who loves us. Belief brings us to a place of relying on God and trusting his care for us. Belief allows us to say along with David, "My help comes from the LORD, who made heaven and earth. He will not let your foot be moved; he who keeps you will not slumber. . . . The LORD is your keeper."[5] When we choose to believe God, we move forward; when we choose to despair, we stay in a pit.

Faith is not just a happy idea for us to think about adding into our lives; it is an essential part of our Christian journey. The Bible tells us, "It is impossible to please God without faith. Anyone who wants to come to him must believe that God exists and that he rewards those who sincerely seek him."[6] We may believe God exists, but do we also believe he rewards those who sincerely seek him? A. W. Tozer put it this way: "It is not enough that we acknowledge God's infinite resources; we must believe also that he is infinitely generous to bestow them."[7]

When we open our hearts to believe that God rewards those who diligently seek him, we begin to open our eyes to his provisions. We begin to see his help in even little ways. Maybe he is blessing us though an encouraging friend, a helping hand with the kids, or an unexpected financial provision. When we don't believe in God as our provider, we tend to think of things as coincidence or chance. We then miss out on the joy of gratitude for a God who loves us. Yes, our spirits are lifted and we begin to thrive as we see his care for us.

C. Change Old, Unhealthy Patterns

As we look to God in faith, we must also humbly recognize that some things may need to change. We must take a candid look at our behavior and turn toward doing what is right. For instance, if we always thought we would be healthy and energetic, yet our bodies are now out of shape and lethargic, we may need to look at a lifestyle change and improve the way we are feeding and taking care of our bodies. Or, if we always thought of ourselves as having a wonderful marriage, but it is loveless because we have become negative, angry, and bitter, then we may need to make some changes in our habits. Or if we never pictured ourselves having financial problems and debt, we may need to look at changes in spending habits or job opportunities.

> *The death of a dream opens up an opportunity for self-evaluation.*

I'm not saying we are responsible for causing all of our own dreams to die, but I am saying it is a good idea to take an honest look at ourselves and see if there is a need for change. Many times we reap what we sow. It's easy to blame others; it's difficult to recognize our own shortcomings or need to do something differently. The death of a dream opens up an opportunity for self-evaluation. We may need to step out of our comfort zones or shyness and meet new people or join a new group. We may need to get rid of an old habit that has slowly become a negative in our lives.

The *C* in this section could also stand for "Confess Your Sin" or "Consult Godly Advice." Both work hand in hand to help us make healthy personal changes. Even David, a man after God's own heart, knew his need for cleansing and renewal as he wrote,

> Purify me from my sins, and I will be clean;
>> wash me, and I will be whiter than snow.
> Oh, give me back my joy again;
>> you have broken me—
>> now let me rejoice.
> Don't keep looking at my sins.
>> Remove the stain of my guilt.
> Create in me a clean heart, O God.
>> Renew a loyal spirit within me.
> Do not banish me from your presence,
>> and don't take your Holy Spirit from me.
>
> Restore to me the joy of your salvation,
>> and make me willing to obey you.[8]

Yes, confession is good for the soul and brings joy to the heart. It is helpful to also seek godly counsel and wisdom as we try to find the beauty in plan B. A wise friend or mentor can help us see areas needing change that we cannot see in ourselves, but we must be open to hearing their words of wisdom. As wise women, we need to always be open to positive change in our lives. I don't think any of us can say we are exactly who we want to be. The book of Proverbs says, "As iron sharpens iron, so a friend sharpens a friend."[9] May we never cease to seek the wise counsel of others in order to be the best we can be.

D. Do What You Can, As You Follow God's Lead

If we are going to thrive in the new plans God has for us, we must first *assess* the possibilities and *believe* God is able to bring hope to our situations. We must *change* and confess any negative habits, but then we must move forward *doing what we can*, as we follow his lead. I'm not saying do everything *you* can; I'm saying, as you follow his leading, do what he leads you to do. Once we open our eyes to the possibilities God is providing, we must take steps forward in faith.

Think about Peter, who boldly stepped out of the boat. Perhaps you are familiar with the story found in chapter 14 of Matthew's gospel. The disciples were in a boat crossing to the other side of the Sea of Galilee, and Jesus decided to join them in a very unconventional way: he walked on the water. When the disciples saw him walking on the water, they were afraid and thought he was a ghost, but Jesus quickly calmed them down and said, "It is I." Can you imagine the fear the disciples felt? They had never seen someone walk on water before. If you are looking at a situation you thought you would never encounter, listen to God's voice saying, *Do not be afraid. I'm right here.*

Peter, in a bold boost of faith, shouts, "Lord, if it is you, tell me to come to you." Jesus said, "Come." Notice Peter wasn't going to step out on the water unless he heard Jesus' invitation to do it. I believe we, too, need to be careful to follow God's leading and listen to him for guidance. We don't need to do everything; we need to do the right things as we step out on faith.

Peter then took the bold move to step out onto the water. He did not wait for Jesus to come push him out of the boat. Where is God calling you to go? What is he inviting you to do? Are you listening to his invitation? Do you see the open door he is providing?

After Peter had stepped out and walked on the water, he took a look at the waves around him and began to sink. Oh no! Didn't he follow God's invitation? How could he possibly be sinking? May I remind you that just because you follow God's guidance doesn't mean you won't face challenges. The lesson we learn from Peter is to turn our eyes back toward Jesus and call out to him. Peter cried, "Lord, save me!" Jesus responded by extending his hand to Peter and helping him up. When you are sinking, look to him, call out to him, and see his hand helping you up.

Look for the help God is providing and the door he is opening. Then take that first step out of the boat and move forward, even if you don't feel like it. Faith is more than a feeling; it is acting on our belief that God is able to bring a redeeming value to any situation. The door he may be opening may not necessarily be what you thought would make you happy or satisfied. It probably does not look like the life you planned for yourself, but trust the Creator of plan B. He has created a beautiful purpose for your life.

Can We Mess Up God's Plan?

In considering the plans God has for us, the question surfaces, "Can our decisions thwart God's ultimate plan for our lives?" Well, I was hoping you wouldn't ask that question. I was hoping to skip merrily through this chapter without addressing the issue of how our choices play out within the sovereignty of God. Since this discussion could take an entire book to answer (and even then the question wouldn't be completely answered), I will only scratch the surface and look at the truth we do know from Scripture.

God in his kindness and goodness has given humans the ability to make choices. We are not robots who only do what we are programmed to do. On the other hand, the Bible tells us we can make our plans but the final results are up to God.[10] David said, "LORD, you have assigned me my portion and my cup; you have made my lot secure."[11] He also said, "The LORD's plans stand firm forever; his intentions can never be shaken."[12] And then later again in the Psalms we read, "The LORD will work out his plans for my life—for your faithful love, O LORD, endures forever."[13] So who is ultimately in charge of our lives, God or us?

We cannot ignore what the Bible reveals about God's sovereignty. For example, in 1 Chronicles we read, "Yours, O LORD, is the greatness, the power, the glory, the victory, and the majesty. Everything in the heavens and on earth is yours, O LORD, and this is your kingdom. We adore you as the one who is over all things. Wealth and honor come from you alone, for you rule over everything. Power and might are in your hand, and at your discretion people are made great and given strength. O our God, we thank you and praise your glorious name!"[14]

Do our poor choices or bad decisions change God's ultimate plan and purpose?

And in the book of Daniel we read,

> His rule is everlasting,
> and his kingdom is eternal.
> All the people of the earth
> are nothing compared to him.
> He does as he pleases
> among the angels of heaven
> and among the people of the earth.
> No one can stop him or say to him,
> "What do you mean by doing these things?"[15]

Do our poor choices or bad decisions change God's ultimate plan and purpose? Or is it possible for someone else's sin or wrongdoing to mess up the blessings God has for us? I don't claim to understand how God rules the affairs of mankind, but I can see from God's Word that he is sovereign. Ultimately he is in charge, and we are not. We can deliberate all we want about our choices versus

God's will, but if we believe what the Bible says about God, then we must conclude that he rules over all the earth and his ultimate plan always prevails.

I Like the Person I Have Become

When we see the good God can bring from any circumstances, and when we begin to passionately live this life we didn't plan, we begin to see things differently. We recognize God's provisions along the way, and we see inklings of blessings in the new plan—a plan that has sprouted from disappointments. Our courage and faith are strengthened in

Had life played out like we had planned, we wouldn't have become who we are today.

the process, as we grow and mature through the challenges. We may even realize that had life played out like we had planned, we wouldn't have become who we are today. That's what Cyndee Hopkins found through her tragic losses.

Cyndee was a devoted wife and mother. Her boys were ages six, four, and almost two when precious little Emma was born. Cyndee's husband, Dave, had just started a new job, and they were all settling into the life of having a baby girl. One night a week later, Dave was tucking the boys into bed and reading them a bedtime story. Cyndee was busy caring for twelve-day-old Emma, but she periodically checked in with the boys to make sure all was going well. When she saw that Dave had fallen asleep with the boys, she decided not to wake him.

The next day when the boys bounded into the kitchen, Cyndee told them to go wake their dad, who was sleeping on the floor at this point. One of the boys reported he was not able to wake his dad. Cyndee went in to try to wake him, and it was then she realized Dave wasn't going to wake up at all. Apparently Dave had suffered a cardiac arrhythmia and had died during the night.

The first year after Dave's death was a blur to Cyndee. Since they had no life insurance, Cyndee depended on the gracious help of others. And help did come: someone anonymously dropped off diapers at her door every few weeks; the family was given a monetary gift from a group of people in a nearby town; and Dave's fraternity brothers started a celebrity golf tournament to raise money for the family. At the time, Cyndee didn't see these as God's provision. She was angry at God and continued to question why her husband had died. But eventually, she recognized that she needed to let go of the questions and move on, not only for her own sake but also to be an example to the kids. She realized that even if God himself came down and told her why he allowed this to happen, it wouldn't change anything.

At the time of Dave's death, Cyndee says her faith was a "holiday faith." She went to church on Easter and Christmas, and that was about it. But she began to feel as though she had an empty spot inside. She started attending church regularly just to have a quiet moment for a few hours on Sunday morning and be around other adults. It was there, sitting in the pew, that she began to receive God's peace and strength in her life. Her faith in Jesus grew to be very real. She was able to look back at the help people gave her and recognize that it was all part of God's provision and care for her and her family.

Several years after Dave passed away, Cyndee noticed that Emma wasn't quite fitting into the circle at preschool like the other kids. She sought help and found that Emma had a high-functioning form of autism. Now Cyndee grieved a different kind of loss. When her husband died, she grieved the loss of a person, but with the diagnosis of a special-needs child, she grieved the loss of the hopes and dreams she had for her daughter. She also grieved every day for the challenges her daughter faced to fit in and feel loved.

As a result of Emma's situation, Cyndee started a website to help and encourage other parents of special-needs kids.[16] She also created a resource book of places to visit and services available for families in the

Dallas/Ft. Worth Metroplex. She helped start a special-needs program at her church and has helped other churches do the same. Cyndee says she felt like a taker after Dave died, but as she grew from her tragedy, God opened her heart with a desire to give back to others. As her kids got older, she decided to serve her community by volunteering as a child advocate in her city.

Cyndee says that although she would have never chosen her challenges, she has learned to be independent and giving through the process. Her unexpected difficulties have been the catalyst to develop qualities in her she never thought she would have. Cyndee is resilient and strong. Her faith in the Lord has grown, and her joy in life has increased. As Cyndee puts it, "I like the person I have become!"

Cyndee's plan B isn't what she would have chosen for her life—plan Bs rarely are. Plan B may not look as pretty as what you hoped your life would look like, yet new and beautiful qualities can emerge in your life as a result. Never underestimate what a redeeming God can do.

STEPPING FORWARD

 ### POINTS

- Plan B may not be your first choice for your life, but it can be a wonderful plan.
- Choose to open your eyes to the beauty of a different plan.
- Prayerfully assess the possibilities God has placed in your life.
- Believe that God is able to bring beauty from ashes.
- Change unhealthy or negative habits.

- Do what you can as you follow God's leading.
- Know that God is sovereign and that we cannot thwart his ultimate plans.
- Find the joy in the new person you have become.

 ## PASSAGE: PSALM 62:1–8

I wait quietly before God,
    for my victory comes from him.
He alone is my rock and my salvation,
    my fortress where I will never be shaken.

So many enemies against one man—
    all of them trying to kill me.
To them I'm just a broken-down wall
    or a tottering fence.
They plan to topple me from my high position.
    They delight in telling lies about me.
They praise me to my face
    but curse me in their hearts.

Let all that I am wait quietly before God,
    for my hope is in him.
He alone is my rock and my salvation,
    my fortress where I will not be shaken.
My victory and honor come from God alone.
    He is my refuge, a rock where no enemy can
        reach me.
O my people, trust in him at all times.
    Pour out your heart to him,
    for God is our refuge.

PRAYER

Mighty and sovereign God, I praise you for you are God Most High. You know all things and can do all things. You are a redeeming God and can create beauty from the rubble of my life. Thank you for your love and care for me. Thank you for your goodness and mercy. Thank you that I can bring my requests to you. Please, Lord, work a miracle in my life. Help me to see the beauty in plan B. Give me strength, wisdom, and resilience. Show me what you want me to do. In Jesus' name, amen.

PLAN

Create a "Beauty in Plan B" journal. Purchase a blank journal and write out the following on the front page:

Beauty in Plan B

A. Assess the possibilities and approach God.
B. Believe he is able. What does the Bible say?
C. Change unhealthy habits, confess sin, consult godly counsel.
D. Do what I can as I follow his leading.

Use this journal to write out what God is showing you in your unexpected journey. It may be a small, unexpected journey as the result of a minor disappointment, or it may be a major life change. Use the ABCD method to direct your thinking and your writing entries. Use this as a place to answer the assessment questions, examine your life, and hear God's voice. Write in it as often as you need to, especially if you are feeling discouraged about the direction of your life. As you look back over the entries, you will be able to see the beauty of your plan-B life emerging.

Our anger and annoyance
are more detrimental to us
than the things themselves which anger or annoy us.

Marcus Aurelius

6

The Bitterness Battle

*Stepping Up to New Responsibilities
and Stepping Away from Anger*

*See to it that no one misses the grace of God
and that no bitter root grows up
to cause trouble and defile many.*

Hebrews 12:15 NIV

THE BITTERNESS GAME is an easy game for women of any age to play. Often it begins with an injustice or unfortunate circumstance, and as the seeds of anger take root, bitter thoughts and attitudes can control our lives. You have heard it said that we can choose to get bitter or to get better. Lynda Hammit chose to get better. I'll let her tell you her story:

My dreams died on October 10, 2000. Allow me to explain. From the time I was a young girl, I wanted to marry a preacher. I loved God with all my heart, and I wanted a man who loved him just as much. Ryan was that man.

After serving with a congregation in Illinois for six years, we were offered the chance to go overseas as full-time missionaries. It took Ryan only one year to raise the support we needed for our family of six to move to East Africa. In 1999, we flew to East Africa to begin a five-year mission commitment in Moshi, Tanzania. Our children were ages fifteen, fourteen, twelve, and ten. We quickly settled into life there in

101

Africa. We had language and culture teachers who worked with us and taught us where to buy what we needed. The children became involved with the international school in Moshi, making new friends and building relationships.

On October 9, 2000, Ryan preached his first sermon in Swahili without the aid of an interpreter. It was a memorable day. The next day we woke up to a gloriously sunny Monday morning. Ryan and I were to drive a native couple to a nearby town so they could catch the bus, while our four children stayed home with a young woman who was interning with us.

This simple trip to the bus station turned our lives upside down. Just as we were crossing a bridge, the truck in front of us blew out a front tire, which caused it to go into the oncoming lane. A bus full of people in the oncoming lane tried to avoid the truck. The truck and the bus hit each other driver to driver, killing both drivers instantly. The bus ricocheted off the truck, swerved into our lane, and hit us head-on. I can still see the bus and truck as they hit, pieces of both vehicles flying through the air, and the bus grill coming straight at us. I have no memory of the impact. Five people died at the scene that day.

When Ryan's head hit the steering wheel, a tear in his brain began bleeding, which caused his brain to swell. The bleeding plus the altitude change while flying for several hours to the hospital in Nairobi made for a disastrous combination. The eventual diagnosis was a closed head injury with moderate to severe brain damage.

In the following days, I had to start making decisions. My husband was now in a coma, and the children were a country away. *Should we go back to the States? Could we just go back home to Tanzania? Would my husband wake up? Who would deal with the children?* So many questions I never dreamed I would have to answer.

Ryan came out of the coma four days later. The doctors diagnosed damage to the frontal lobe and the left part of the brain, causing aphasia (loss of language) and right-side altered feeling. My husband could no longer speak, read, write, or do math. As the doctors gauged his condition, it became apparent that we would need to go back to the States.

When we returned, churches stepped up and helped us get furniture and food. My parents provided a house. God supplied our needs through his people. I was thankful our kids could see the example of God's people working together to help in time of need.

What does a diagnosis of moderate to severe brain damage mean when the rubber hits the road? It means that my husband, a man who had the gifts of persuasive speech and strong decision-making skills, now has extreme difficulties with even the simplest communications. To this day he can't write a check or read a magazine, newspaper, or menu at a restaurant, and he will always tend toward feeling cold. He has trouble keeping up with any conversation and then speaking his thoughts. It also means that I have to navigate the tough waters of dealing with a brain-damaged man with a very strong personality.

For years, time was measured from the day of the accident. After the accident this . . . , after the accident that . . . It seemed to be the start of all time. We finally had to realize we are *not* going back to normal; things will *never* be the same again. In those terrible years, I learned to hide the incredible pain and wear a mask. But wearing the mask did not teach me how to live this new life. I felt like my life was one failure after another: I didn't know how to be a wife to this now depressed, angry, frustrated man. I had children who were confused and angry at the changes in their lives, a church family who only saw us as we had been, and counselors who wanted to know what we wanted fixed. I dealt with Social Security to get disability and banks to pay our bills. Pain filled my whole world.

Our pain was not obvious for all to see; we looked the same on the outside. We moved back to the town where Ryan had preached, hoping to ease the transition with things that were familiar. I now realize that the reason we could not succeed was that I was trying to stay in a life we no longer had access to. I kept trying to put back the broken puzzle pieces of the life we had before the accident, and it was not to be.

In desperation I prayed, "Father, I need you to move us. We are dying in this place. I will trust you if you say no, but I really need you to move us. I need you to move us in the next two weeks." I know, I know, my husband thought I was crazy too. I'm not sure you should give God a time limit; however, school started in two weeks, and two of the children were still in school. It was important to me that they begin a new school on the first day. I prayed that my family would be put in a position to succeed with a new start.

We examined several possibilities, and I knew that if God had a place in mind, he would make it happen. Two weeks to the day of that prayer, we pulled our moving van loaded with all our possessions into West Monroe, Louisiana. God provided a place for my husband to work as a groundskeeper at a camp just outside West Monroe, and he did

> *Lynda turned her despair into hope and expectancy, as she took her eyes off her old dreams and placed them on the Lord.*

it in *two weeks*. The children started school on Monday, two days after our arrival. God had answered our prayers. Even though neither my husband nor our children wanted to make the move, they will all tell you today that it was the best move we ever made.

It has now been over seven years since the accident. I rarely measure time by it anymore. We have an incredible church home, wonderful friends, and a new life that I never thought possible. My dreams may have died on October 10, 2000, but God raised us from the ashes of pain and gave us a new life.

It's not the life I dreamed I would have, but it could have been a lot worse if I had allowed roots of bitterness and anger to grow in my heart. God heard my cry for help and worked it together for good; he brought us into a new world of life and hope. I praise his name with my whole heart.

I asked Lynda to share her story because she reminds us that we have choices when it comes to the unchosen challenges of life.

We can stew in self-pity and anger, or we can step up to the new responsibilities. We also have a choice in attitude. Sometimes when we are forced into new responsibilities, we kick and scream the whole way. Lynda turned her despair into hope and expectancy, as she took her eyes off her old dreams and placed them on the Lord.

The Ugliness of Bitterness

We all have a tendency to hold on to old expectations and hopes. It's difficult to adjust when life takes us down unexpected roads. We may even feel entitled to a less-complicated life or a better husband or a more dignified job. When a disconnect occurs between our expectations and reality, we can begin to develop frustration and anger. If we feed those feelings, over time they can grow into roots of bitterness.

Bitterness is like an infectious disease that plagues our lives if we let it. The symptoms are numerous and typically easy to identify. A hardened or hurt countenance, blaming and condemning conversations, and a negative and unforgiving spirit are just a few of the ugly symptoms. Of course, some people are pretty good at masking the symptoms. There are those who harbor bitter thoughts but never let anyone know. The problem is, whether you let people in on your battle with bitterness or not, it is still painfully detrimental to your life.

> *Bitterness not only affects what you say and how you think, but it can literally affect you physically.*

Bitterness is an unbecoming disease. It not only affects what you say and how you think, but it can literally affect you physically. High blood pressure and heart disease are among the maladies linked to bitterness and anger. Perhaps the ugliest result of a bitter spirit is the effect it has on relationships. Family members and friends do not tend to enjoy the company of a negative person.

I don't know about you, but when I want to get together with friends, I would much rather call Upbeat Beth than Bitter Betty.

You have heard that misery loves company, and that is true. The Bitter Betty Bunch may choose to sit around and ruminate about their troubles, enjoying their pity parties. But we must move forward and allow God to take us in a new direction, blessing other people in the process. Basically, bitterness is a selfish pool in which to drown our sorrows. It prevents us from experiencing a meaningful life. Instead of helping others, bitter attitudes only bring others down. When my life here on earth is over, I hope people will be able to say I helped them have a better life. When we bring joy to others and help them along life's way, our life is rich and meaningful. But if we live our lives in bitterness and anger, what benefit is that to this world?

> *Anger is not a sin. It is a feeling that surfaces in our emotions when we recognize that an injustice has taken place.*

Handling Our Anger Wisely

When we harbor anger in our hearts, it grows into that nasty disease of bitterness. So what do you do when you have the first signs of anger? Go to the doctor. The Great Physician offers us a prescription for peace and healing. Let's take a look at his Manual for a Healthy Life (the Bible) and learn from him.

Before we get started, I believe we need to understand one important point: anger is not a sin. Does that surprise you? Anger is a feeling that surfaces in our emotions when we recognize an injustice has taken place. Frustration and anger happen quite naturally, but it's what we do with the anger that makes a difference in our lives and in the lives of others.

The apostle Paul gives us specific details about how to handle anger. He instructs, "'Don't sin by letting anger control you.' Don't let the sun go down while you are still angry, for anger gives a foothold to the devil."[1] When we experience anger, Paul says, don't let it control you or get the best of you. Recognize it early and get rid of it. Keep short accounts. In other words, don't harbor your anger and allow it to grow. Now how do we do that? Paul tells us later in this same passage, "Get rid of all bitterness, rage, anger, harsh words, and slander, as well as all types of evil behavior. Instead, be kind to each other, tenderhearted, forgiving one another, just as God through Christ has forgiven you."[2]

Bitterness, rage, harsh words, and slander are all examples of anger turning into sin. So when we are frustrated and feel as though an injustice has taken place, we need to switch gears. Rather than allowing bitterness to grow, we need to be kind, tenderhearted, and forgiving. *What!* you might be saying to yourself. *Are you kidding!? That's just the opposite of what I want to do! How in the world do I get there?* May I suggest two ways: by looking at Christ's example and by asking for his help.

You see, if anyone was treated unjustly, it was Jesus himself. He was perfect, he was love, and he did no wrong; yet his enemies crucified him and his friend betrayed him. He certainly had a reason to be angry on that cross, but instead of shouting, "Don't you know I'm doing this for you!" he said, "Father, forgive them, for they don't know what they are doing."[3] Jesus lived in a spirit of forgiveness, and he tells us over and over to forgive others. Here's how he told us to handle injustice:

> I tell you who hear me: Love your enemies, do good to those who hate you, bless those who curse you, pray for those who mistreat you. If someone strikes you on one cheek, turn to him the other also. If someone takes your cloak, do not stop him from taking your tunic. Give to

everyone who asks you, and if anyone takes what belongs
to you, do not demand it back. Do to others as you
would have them do to you.

If you love those who love you, what credit is that to
you? Even "sinners" love those who love them. And if
you do good to those who are good to you, what credit
is that to you? Even "sinners" do that. And if you lend to
those from whom you expect repayment, what credit
is that to you? Even "sinners" lend to "sinners," expecting
to be repaid in full. But love your enemies, do good to
them, and lend to them without expecting to get
anything back. Then your reward will be great, and you
will be sons of the Most High, because he is kind to the
ungrateful and wicked. Be merciful, just as your Father is
merciful.

Do not judge, and you will not be judged. Do not
condemn, and you will not be condemned. Forgive, and
you will be forgiven. Give, and it will be given to you. A
good measure, pressed down, shaken together and
running over, will be poured into your lap. For with the
measure you use, it will be measured to you.[4]

Did you notice what Jesus said about your right to harbor bitterness and resentment? What about when we think we are sup-
posed to get back at people with our anger? What about self-pity?
Rage? Those aren't there either. Jesus tells us that instead of fuel-
ing our anger, we need to love and forgive. I will make one side
note: this passage is not referring to abusive spouses. Please protect yourself and your children if you are in a dangerous situation.
Certainly we must set healthy boundaries in any type of unhealthy
relationship.

NEW THOUGHTS = NEW YOU

The irresponsibility of Katie's ex-husband left her with two kids and a large debt. It was tempting for her to allow anger and bitterness to grow. She wanted to make him pay up and own up to his responsibilities, but eventually she realized he never would. So she chose to step away from the place of anger and move forward with her new responsibilities. It wasn't necessarily what she wanted to do. This was not in her plan for life, but when she finally let go of those old dreams and accepted her new reality, she began to move forward.

Katie has made a good life for herself and her kids, despite the challenges. She is an active volunteer at her kids' school and blesses others through both her work and her friendships. She says that when she began to let go of the past and step up to her new place in life, she became a new woman, a woman who is relying on God and thriving in the plan B of her life.

Do you feel entitled to bitterness in any area of your life right now? Katie's story offers a good example of fading out of bitterness and into a new life. Whether it is toward God or toward others, you can choose what you will do with your anger and bitterness. We learned from Jesus to replace anger with love. Pray for our enemies and do good to them. When we begin to pray for our enemies, our hearts begin to change. Anger subsides as we give our hurts to the Father and sincerely pray for those who hurt us. I want to encourage you to try it and then watch what God begins to do in your heart. The bars of bitterness that enslave you will begin to melt. Sometimes it is hard to forgive because it seems like you are letting the other person off the hook. Forgiveness doesn't mean you allow someone to walk all over you or let him get away with terrible things. Forgiveness means you re-

> *Sometimes it is hard to forgive because it seems like you are letting the other person off the hook.*

lease the right to hold the offense over the other person. Forgiveness frees you from the battle raging within your heart.

The Bible tells us that God brings righteousness and justice to all who are oppressed.[5] Are you willing to trust God to carry out justice? Are you willing to leave it in his hands? Anger and bitterness will not bring forth justice; they will ruin your life and prevent you from moving forward. When we live in forgiveness, we live in freedom. Certainly you must set wise and healthy boundaries if someone hurts you. Forgiveness is not allowing someone to continue in a destructive behavior, nor is it allowing someone to get away without consequences. Forgiveness is an act of the will, releasing the right to hold something against a person in your heart.

Forgiveness begins to move us away from the battle of bitterness, but we must also come to the point of accepting the fact that our lives have possibly changed. Acceptance means letting go of our old dreams and recognizing that our lives are starting new and different chapters. I know this is difficult, because it means we are saying good-bye to the things we knew. I encourage you to talk about your pain in letting go of bitterness with a friend or even a counselor. Write it out in a journal. Admit the disappointment and hurt you feel as you close the old chapters of your life. The longer you hold on to the unfairness of the situation and avoid acceptance, the more opportunity you give for bitterness to grow.

The battle with bitterness takes place in our minds. When our thoughts are consumed with resentment, we fight a losing battle. Forgiving others and releasing the resentment is nearly impossible in human terms, but with God all things are possible.

My friend, if you feel as though you just can't forgive and move on, talk to the One who showed ultimate forgiveness. He will help you. Through Christ's death on the cross, we are forgiven of all our sins—not some of them, but all. As those who are forgiven, we in turn must not harbor unforgiveness and bitterness toward others. Possibly one of the most joyful and freeing phrases in the

Bible are these powerful few words, "Forgive as the Lord forgave you."[6]

Jesus taught us to be proactive when it comes to dealing with our enemies. As we read earlier, Jesus told us to love them, do good to them, bless them, and pray for them. We begin to have victory in our battle with bitterness when we have a change in heart and begin to follow Jesus' words. I know, I know, that's not what you wanted to hear. Actually when Jesus said these words, many people turned away from following him because these are tough words. Are you up for the challenge? Let's ask God to help us love our enemies, do good to them, and pray for them. As the bitterness is blown away, we will find joy thriving and blooming in its place!

STEPPING FORWARD

 ### POINTS

- When we hold on to anger and resentment, we allow the roots of bitterness to grow.
- Bitterness is an ugly disease that can ruin our lives.
- We have a choice in how we handle our anger.
- Jesus told us to love our enemies, do good to them, bless them, and pray for them.
- Forgive as the Lord forgave you.
- Forgiveness doesn't mean you give someone the right to hurt you again.
- Go to the Great Physician for healing and help.

 ### PASSAGE: COLOSSIANS 3:1–4, 8–15

Since you have been raised to new life with Christ, set your sights on the realities of heaven, where Christ sits in the place of honor at God's right hand. Think about the things of heaven, not the things of earth. For you died to this life, and your real life is hidden with Christ in God. And when Christ, who is your life, is revealed to the whole world, you will share in all his glory. . . .

Now is the time to get rid of anger, rage, malicious behavior, slander, and dirty language. Don't lie to each other, for you have stripped off your old sinful nature and all its wicked deeds. Put on your new nature, and be renewed as you learn to know your Creator and become like him. In this new life, it doesn't matter if you are a Jew or a Gentile, circumcised or uncircumcised, barbaric, uncivilized, slave, or free. Christ is all that matters, and he lives in all of us.

Since God chose you to be the holy people he loves, you must clothe yourselves with tenderhearted mercy, kindness, humility, gentleness, and patience. Make allowance for each other's faults, and forgive anyone who offends you.

Remember, the Lord forgave you, so you must forgive others. Above all, clothe yourselves with love, which binds us all together in perfect harmony. And let the peace that comes from Christ rule in your hearts. For as members of one body you are called to live in peace. And always be thankful.

 PRAYER

Holy and just heavenly Father, I praise you for your kindness and mercy toward me. Thank you for forgiving me of all my sins through Jesus. Thank you for showing us what forgiveness looks like. Help me to forgive. Heal my bitterness as I begin to accept my new situation. Show me what I am equipped to do, and give me the strength to take positive steps forward. Use me to encourage and uplift others. Restore my joy. In Jesus' name, amen.

 ## PLAN

Do a bitterness check. Ask yourself the following questions:

- Is there anyone I need to forgive?
- Am I mad at God?
- Am I holding on to old dreams and expectations?
- Am I focused solely on myself and my situation?
- Am I stuck in a rut, refusing to look at positive options?

If you answered yes to any of the above, I encourage you to prayerfully ask God to heal your heart and help you forgive. Remember, he is really good at that! Ask him to help you let go of the hurt and discover the joy of forgiveness. In God's strength, look for ways to love your enemies and do good to them. And don't forget to pray for them.

The humble will see their God at work and be glad.
Let all who seek God's help be encouraged.

Psalm 69:32

7

Big-Picture Thinking

Renewing Your Focus Can Revive Your Spirit

*One thought of eternity
makes all earthly sorrow fade away.*

Basilea Schlink

Robin Hiser is a high-functioning Down syndrome woman in her fifties who has a deep and abiding love for the Lord. She lifts others up through her encouraging words and genuine love for people, and she gives God all the glory. Robin recognizes the value of every person and sees each one as a creation of God and a part of his handiwork. Although she admits it is difficult for her when some people look down on her because she looks and talks differently, she knows God created her for a special purpose.

Robin loves to worship the Lord and read her Bible. In fact, she inspires others to a deeper faith and desire to walk with God in simplicity and truth. She says her greatest joy will be when one day she enters heaven and Jesus hugs her, saying, "Well done, good and faithful servant."

Until then, she has work to do here on earth and serves God wherever he leads her. Robin's life is rich and meaningful because of her eternal perspective. She has a joyful outlook because she is living her life with a wide-angle lens. She is not living for this world; she is living for God's kingdom.

Robin's story reminds me of how important our perspective in life is in relation to our day-to-day struggles. If we are living and working for only this life and the here and now, we can easily grow discouraged, tired, and even depressed. But when we recognize that God can use our difficulties and disabilities in a special purpose, we see glimpses of hope that can grow into joy. No matter what limitations we have or how difficult our situation is, we can still bloom and thrive in a life used by God.

Where is your focus? Is it on what's wrong in your life, or is it on a big God who is able to bring meaning to your life? Are you consumed with the miserable situation you are in now, or are you looking with expectation to the bigger picture of what God can do? Our focus makes a difference in our attitudes and actions.

HAVING EYES FOR ETERNITY

On July 4, 1952, Florence Chadwick set out to be the first woman to swim the twenty-six-mile stretch from Catalina Island to the California coast. With national camera crews and her family by her side, Florence began her incredible feat in the icy cold waters. When sharks hovered around her, her support crew fired rifles to scare them away. Florence had already made history by being the first woman to swim the English Channel, and she was expected to make this goal as well, since she had already proven her persistence and ability.

Unfortunately, a deep, dense fog developed over the water, making it nearly impossible for Florence to see anything in front of her including the coastline. As her family and crew cheered her on, all she could see was the fog. After fifteen hours, she still couldn't see the end in sight and became defeated. Numbed by the cold, Florence asked to be taken out of the water. Sadly, once Florence was in the comfort of the boat, she found out that she only had half a mile to complete her goal. Later in an interview with a reporter she said, "Look, I'm not excusing myself. But if I could have seen land, I might have made it."[1]

Florence later reflected that it wasn't the cold or the fatigue that made her give up; the fog alone had defeated her because it kept her from seeing her goal. Two months later Florence gave it another try, and the fog was there again. But this time Florence was prepared for it. She trained herself to concentrate only on her goal and not on the fog. As she swam, she kept reminding herself that the fog didn't change the end result and the fact the shoreline was there, whether she could see it or not. She knew if she remained faithful to continue swimming, she would reach the shore. And she did! She not only forged through the fog; she also broke the all-time speed record by two full hours, a record previously set by a man![2]

What made the difference? Focus. On her second try, Florence chose to focus on her end goal even though she couldn't see it. She chose to deliberately keep her focus off of the fog in front of her. What an incredible life lesson for us as Christians. The challenges and cares of this world tend to cloud our view of eternity. Yet when we fix our focus on heaven as our end goal, we begin to see how temporary our challenges are here on this earth. Yes, it is easy to get distracted by the fog of frustrations and disappointments in our lives; but like Florence, we must continue to persevere with our focus on the bigger picture of eternity.

The writer of Hebrews encourages us in this way:

Since we are surrounded by such a huge crowd of witnesses to the life of faith, let us strip off every weight that slows us down, especially the sin that so easily trips us up. And let us run with endurance the race God has set before us. We do this by keeping our eyes on Jesus, the champion who initiates and perfects our faith. Because of the joy awaiting him, he endured the cross, disregarding its shame. Now he is seated in the place of honor beside God's throne. Think of all the hostility he endured from sinful people; then you won't become weary and give up.[3]

The Power of Meditation

Practically speaking, how do we keep our minds continually fixed on Jesus and eternity and remember that our lives here on earth are temporary? How do we keep ourselves from being consumed by the cares of this world? One way to set our minds on things above is to meditate on who God is, what he has done, and what he has to say to his followers. When we contemplate and reflect on the Bible, we can't help but encourage our minds in thinking about eternity.

God desires for us to meditate on his Word. In the Old Testament, we read his words to Joshua who was about to lead the Israelites into the Promised Land. Now this was no easy task. Even God called the Israelites a "stubborn people."[4] Imagine Joshua's job description: "Must be able to lead thousands of ornery, cantankerous, stubborn, discontented people into a new land. Must be able to organize them and lead them into numerous battles in which they will be outsized and outnumbered." I don't know about you, but I wouldn't want the job.

Without a doubt, Joshua needed to keep his eyes on the Lord. His faith needed to be strong, and he needed to constantly remember that God had already promised that he would bring the Israelites into a new and wonderful land. It was of necessity that Joshua keep his eyes on the big picture and not get caught up in the fear of the lesser challenges along the way. So what advice did God give Joshua to help him keep his faith-filled perspective? Here it is: "Do not let this Book of the Law depart from your mouth; meditate on it day and night, so that you may be careful to do everything written in it. Then you will be prosperous and successful. Have I not commanded you? Be strong and courageous. Do not be terrified; do not be discouraged, for the LORD your God will be with you wherever you go."[5]

If Joshua needed those words for his major battles, I believe we could use the same dose of encouragement for our personal battles. Meditating on God's Word means reflecting upon it, pondering it, and considering what God is teaching us through it. As we meditate on God's Word, we become transformed by the renewing of our minds. We are reminded and encouraged that there is a bigger

> *Meditating on God's Word brings a cup of refreshing water to our parched and thirsty souls.*

picture and our sovereign God has our lives in his hands. Meditating on God's Word brings a cup of refreshing water to our parched and thirsty souls.

Joyce Huggett, an internationally known writer, speaker, and broadcaster based in Cyprus, wrote the following words about meditation:

> We meditate to give God's words the opportunity to penetrate, not just our minds, but our emotions—the places where we hurt—and our will—the place where we make choices and decisions. We meditate to encounter the Living Word, Jesus himself. We meditate so that every part of our being, our thoughts and our affections and our ambitions, are turned to face and honor and glorify him. Yet another reason for learning to meditate is so that we may become conversant with the will of God.[6]

As we meditate on God's Word and allow it to seep into our hearts and minds, we get a glimpse of the fact that God has a magnificent plan for humanity. It began in the Garden of Eden and has been playing out ever since. What may look like a tragedy or mistake is part of a bigger and broader picture. If we only focus on one part, we miss the beauty of the whole. For instance, Christ's death on the cross in and of itself was a horrible thing, but in light of eternity, it is the most passionate picture of love the world could ever imagine.

The Beauty of Contemplation

For me personally, meditating on God's Word has made a tangible difference in the way I view life. When I reflect on the Old Testament, reading stories of God's provision for his people in the wilderness or God's help in overcoming enemies, I find myself encouraged that God is able to handle any challenge I face. In the New Testament, as I read about Jesus taking a small lunch and feeding thousands, I'm reminded that he can take what little I have to offer and do great things. As I read about Paul's transformation, I realize that God can grab a life headed in the wrong direction, turn it around, and use it for a divine and powerful purpose.

Yes, meditating on God's Word changes my ordinary thinking into extraordinary thinking. My petty thoughts become hope-filled thoughts, and my despair about what's happening now changes into the joy of what is to come. I begin to see possibilities when I read, "With God all things are possible."[7] There is a renewed focus of eternity when I ponder Paul's words: "To live is Christ and to die is gain."[8] One particular way I have found to meditate on God's Word is a process called *lectio divina.*

> *Meditating on God's Word changes my ordinary thinking into extraordinary thinking.*

Lectio divina is a Latin term for sacred or divine reading and is a meaningful way to reflect on God's Word. Richard Foster describes it this way: "The practice of *Lectio Divina* has been a long and time-honored history among the people of God. It was important for Christians many centuries ago because they knew they needed to come to Scripture for life and for the transformation of the human personality. That is exactly why we need to learn it again today."[9] Although it is a centuries-old practice, *lectio divina* offers even the modern-day follower an enriching and reflective way to contemplate the Scriptures.

In their book *Be Still*, Judge and Amy Reinhold tell us, "*Lectio Divina* is a slow, deliberate reading and meditation on Scripture. It begins with developing the ability to listen deeply. We must first learn to be silent in order to hear the 'still small voice of God.'"[10] I highly recommend their book, which leads you to a deeper meditative prayer life as you listen and ponder God's Word. There is no right or wrong way to practice *lectio divina*. The following introduction to the process of *lectio divina* comes from the Benedictine monks of Saint Andrews Abbey in Valyermo, California:[11] They suggest:

> *"Lectio Divina is a slow, deliberate reading and meditation on Scripture."*
> —Be Still

1. Choose a text of the Scriptures that you wish to pray.
2. Place yourself in a comfortable position and allow yourself to become silent.
3. Turn to the text and read it slowly, gently.
4. Next take the word or phrase into yourself. Memorize or repeat the passage.
5. Speak to God. Respond to Him in prayer.
6. Finally, simply rest in God's embrace.

They add, "Sometimes in *lectio divina* one will return several times to the printed text, either to savor the literary context of the word or phrase that God has given, or to seek a new word or phrase to ponder. At other times only a single word or phrase will fill the whole time set aside for *lectio divina*. It is not necessary to anxiously assess the quality of one's *lectio divina* as if one were 'performing' or seeking some goal: *lectio divina* has no goal other than that of being in the presence of God by praying the Scriptures."

For me personally, I like to take a passage of Scripture and read it four times aloud, listening and taking in his Word. I usually write out my thoughts in a journal answering two questions: (1) What is God teaching through this particular passage? and (2) What do I personally learn through these words?

Certainly *lectio divina* is not the only method of gaining a more heavenly perspective on life, but it is one way to meditate on God's Word. The point of contemplating the Scriptures through meditation and memorization is to turn our hearts and minds toward eternity. Much of what we see around us in the way of advertisements and promotions compels us to be enthralled by this world and the here and now. It takes an intentional transformation of the way we think to live for a better land, our heavenly kingdom. When our minds are dwelling on the things of this world, limitations and disappointments will loom large. But if our eyes are on the Lord's work and a greater purpose, the situations of earth begin to grow strangely dim.

EYES THAT SEE BEYOND

In the middle of the city of Chandigarh, India, sits a quite unusual garden. It is an amazing testament to the artistic value of trash. That's right, trash. Celebrated artist Nek Chand used materials people discarded as trash and formed them into an artistic wonder called the Rock Garden. Chand considers it an expression of his hope for humanity. While others may look at trash as a problem that needs to be hidden away, the artist saw it in a different way. He saw the trash as objects that could be creatively transformed into art.

"It all started out of personal curiosity," says Chand, who started building the garden in the 1950s using urban and industrial waste. He began by clearing a little patch of jungle in order to create a small garden area for himself. He collected boulders, metal pieces, lag stones, overburned bricks, broken pots, chinaware, rags, plastic dolls, battered hats, broken bangles, shoes, bottles, you name it! All of it was used in his work to transform trash into a grand mosaic of treasure and beauty. There was no limit to what he could envision and create out of the trash.

Gradually his creative art display developed and grew, eventually covering several acres that displayed hundreds of sculptures. For the first eighteen years of his project, he had to work in the secrecy of night, fearing he would be discovered by the authorities. In fact, when the government officials did discover the garden, they were confused as to how to handle the situation. The art garden was illegally built on a forbidden area, which meant they had the right to demolish it, but they recognized its beautiful and unique qualities. So instead of demolishing the sculpture garden, the city decided to give Chand a salary to allow him to work on the garden full-time. They even provided a workforce of fifty laborers. The garden was finally opened to the public in 1976. Today there are more than twenty-five acres with thousands of sculptures set in large mosaic courtyards, linked by walled paths and deep gorges. There is also a series of interlinking waterfalls.

The Rock Garden is now admired as one of the modern wonders of the world and is considered one of the greatest artistic achievements seen in India since the Taj Mahal. Currently they have more than five thousand visitors a day. Carl Lindquist, who works with the international program at Arkansas State University, described it this way, "Built of industrial waste and thrown-away items, the Rock Garden in the city of Chandigarh is perhaps the world's most poignant and salient statement of the possibility of finding beauty in the unexpected and accidental."[12]

Amazing! Objects that were once considered trash were turned into a beautiful work of art. I love Lindquist's phrase "finding beauty in the unexpected and accidental." Nek Chand didn't see trash; he saw treasure. That's what God sees in our lives! He holds the broken pieces of our lives in his hands and fits

> *We may see a mess here, a mistake there, a tragic loss, or an unfortunate incident, but God sees potential.*

them into a beautiful mosaic for eternity. We may see a mess here, a mistake there, a tragic loss, or an unfortunate incident, but God sees potential. Singularly a piece of trash isn't so lovely, but like Chand, God sees the wonderful work that can be formed. As we draw close to him and hear his voice, we begin to hear the whisper of the Master Artist saying, *Trust me. I can make something good come from this.*

Open Our Eyes, Lord

Let's ask God to give us eyes to see beyond our circumstances. I'm reminded of the story we read about Elisha in 2 Kings 6. When Elisha and his servant were surrounded by enemy troops, Elisha's servant needed a little reassurance that God was with them. It is such a powerful story, I want you to read it for yourself:

> One night the king of Aram sent a great army with many chariots and horses to surround the city.
>
> When the servant of the man of God got up early the next morning and went outside, there were troops, horses, and chariots everywhere. "Oh, sir, what will we do now?" the young man cried to Elisha.
>
> "Don't be afraid!" Elisha told him. "For there are more on our side than on theirs!" Then Elisha prayed, "O LORD, open his eyes and let him see!" The LORD opened the young man's eyes, and when he looked up, he saw that the hillside around Elisha was filled with horses and chariots of fire.[13]

Isn't that an amazing story? Can't you relate to Elisha's servant as he saw the great army and exclaimed, "What will we do now?" Perhaps you have exclaimed those same words. How kind of God to open the servant's eyes to see the chariots of fire that filled the hillside! Ironically, God closed the eyes of the Aramean army, and Elisha led them away blind into the city of Samaria and into the hand of the king of Israel. Isn't that interesting? God opened the eyes of one and shut the eyes of others. We may not see chariots of fire, but God can open our eyes to a broader perspective. He can open our eyes to see the treasures waiting to be discovered in our new place. He can show us the possibilities and potential that exist all around us.

OUR LIVES, HIS WORK

Autumn Ater has treasure focus. If you met her, you would find a joyful and thankful woman, but her life hasn't been easy. Her son, Robert, was born with multiple disabilities, not able to walk or talk. Autumn felt she was blessed with the special mission of caring for her son. She soon realized that Robert was sent to her to teach her about love and enjoying the simple pleasures of life. Robert went on to his heavenly home two years ago at the young age of fourteen, but Autumn lives with a unique perspective. She says, "Although Robert has been gone for two years, I look at it as being two years closer to when I'll be with him again in heaven."

After Robert's death, Autumn started a ministry to help other grieving moms. She named it A Hole in My Heart Ministries. Her mission is to reach out to bereaved mothers with God's Word and offer comfort and understanding for their hurting hearts. She says, "Turn your moments into memories by allowing God's healing light to shine into the hole of a mother's broken heart, where mending can begin to take place. We cannot let our grief, painful as it is, become our identity. We are much more than that. . . . Our children want us to be so much more than that!"[14]

Autumn knows that she was put on this earth to be a vessel of God's love and to help mothers who are hurting due to the death of a child. Autumn's focus was much broader than being the caregiver for a disabled child or a mother of a deceased son. Those descriptions were certainly a part of her journey, but they are not her whole identity. Her eyes are focused on a God who loves her and has a plan for her here on this earth until she goes to see her Savior and hug her son in their eternal home.

God picked up the broken pieces in Autumn's life and put together a beautiful vessel of his love. What can God do through the broken pieces of your life? You may not be able to see the whole picture right now, but God is creating a beautiful mosaic piece by piece. If we look at the individual pieces of a mosaic design, they may not look so lovely. Yet when we step back and examine the whole picture, we see a wonderful work of art fashioned by the Creator's hands. You were created for beauty; you were created for joyful living; you were created to thrive, not simply survive!

STEPPING FORWARD

 ### POINTS

- Our focus makes a difference in our actions and attitude.
- It is easy for us to become consumed with the here and now and forget to step back to see the bigger picture.
- We find hope and strength in God's Word.
- Meditate on God's Word to maintain an eternal perspective in life.
- Ask God to open your eyes to possibilities and potential in both circumstances and people.
- The broken pieces of our lives may not be pretty,

but they can come together in a beautiful mosaic designed by our Creator.

 PASSAGE: PSALM 119:25–40

I lie in the dust;
    revive me by your word.
I told you my plans, and you answered.
    Now teach me your decrees.
Help me understand the meaning of your
    commandments,
    and I will meditate on your wonderful deeds.
I weep with sorrow;
    encourage me by your word.
Keep me from lying to myself;
    give me the privilege of knowing your instructions.
I have chosen to be faithful;
    I have determined to live by your regulations.
I cling to your laws.
    Lord, don't let me be put to shame!
I will pursue your commands,
    for you expand my understanding.

Teach me your decrees, O Lord;
    I will keep them to the end.
Give me understanding and I will obey your instructions;
    I will put them into practice with all my heart.
Make me walk along the path of your commands,
    for that is where my happiness is found.
Give me an eagerness for your laws
    rather than a love for money!
Turn my eyes from worthless things,
    and give me life through your word.

Reassure me of your promise,
    made to those who fear you.
Help me abandon my shameful ways;
    for your regulations are good.
I long to obey your commandments!
    Renew my life with your goodness.

PRAYER

Eternal Father, loving God, I praise you that you hold all things in your hands. You are preparing us for eternity, and you have a beautiful purpose for our lives. Thank you for your plan that goes far beyond what I can ask or imagine. Keep me focused on you, and help me to always keep in mind the bigger eternal picture. Help me to abide in your words and dwell in your loving embrace. Turn me from my small and self-centered viewpoint, so that I may see my situation with hope-filled eternal eyes. In Jesus' name, amen.

PLAN

Write the following verses on index cards and display them in places where you will see them often (refrigerator, car, makeup mirror, computer). Choose one to memorize, or you may want to memorize them all. Come on, you can do it! Each verse serves as a tremendous reminder for us to keep our eyes on the eternal picture.

Ecclesiastes 3:11—God has made everything beautiful for its own time. He has planted eternity in the human heart, but even so, people cannot see the whole scope of God's work from beginning to end.

2 Corinthians 4:18—We don't look at the troubles we can see now; rather, we fix our gaze on things that cannot be seen. For the things we see now will soon be gone, but the things we cannot see will last forever.

Colossians 3:1—Since you have been raised to new life with Christ, set your sights on the realities of heaven, where Christ sits in the place of honor at God's right hand.

1 Peter 4:12–13—Dear friends, don't be surprised at the fiery trials you are going through, as if something strange were happening to you. Instead, be very glad—for these trials make you partners with Christ in his suffering, so that you will have the wonderful joy of seeing his glory when it is revealed to all the world.

Our words are the evidence of the state of our hearts
as surely as the taste of the water
is an evidence of the state of the spring.

J. C. Ryle

8

You Are What You Say

Speaking with Sincerity rather than Complaining

*May the words of my mouth
and the meditation of my heart
be pleasing to you,
O LORD, my rock and my redeemer.*

Psalm 19:14

Linda is one of the most loving and giving people I know. She brings cheer to others through her smile and lifts others through her words of encouragement. It is easy to assume that a beautiful and confident person like Linda must have had everything in life go her way, but the truth is, Linda has had a few twists and turns in her journey.

In one of the hottest summers Dallas ever experienced, Linda's car burst into flames as a result of overheating and paint fumes in her garage. Linda was inside the house talking with her sister, while Linda's six-month-old daughter Holly lay in her crib napping. When the two sisters began to notice smoke, they searched out the source and found that their house as well as the neighbor's house was on fire. Everyone was able to get out safely as they watched the entire house go up in flames in less than thirty minutes. They lost everything, but Linda and her husband, Jerry, had strong spirits and wonderful friends. They began to rebuild their lives slowly but surely.

Seven years later, their second daughter, Paige, was born with a cleft lip and palate. Her first surgery was done at the tender age of three months, followed by another significant one when Paige was one year old. Linda estimates Paige has had more than fifteen surgeries and has been a trooper through them all. Linda's care and unconditional love for Paige has helped Paige grow to be a thriving young lady herself. But that's not the end of Linda's story.

When Paige was seventeen, an electrical problem in the attic caused yet another fire in their home. This time the firemen were able to salvage much of their pictures and furniture, although the house itself had to be completely rebuilt. Linda, in her typical upbeat fashion, just threw up her hands and said, "Not again!" Linda and Jerry have had to bounce back and rebuild twice, and Jerry has been a tremendous leader and support for the family.

A person who has had two houses burn to the ground and watched their daughter go through surgery after surgery may be a little bitter or angry. Not Linda! She finds her strength from God and continually looks for ways she can serve and give back to others. Her list of volunteer service in the Dallas community is a mile long, from volunteering and serving on the board of Children's Medical Center to giving her time to the Women's Guild of United Cerebral Palsy.

She has blessed the people at her church by teaching Sunday school and planning birthday parties for elderly members of the congregation. Linda has a heart for college girls and for the unborn, so she gives her time to meet with young women who are considering having an abortion. The most beautiful blessing is to see the gracious love Linda's daughters have toward others. Both girls are lovely reflections of their mother, who has discovered the joy that comes from encouraging others through her words and reaching out to lift another person through her actions.

Our Words Define Us

Linda is known by her friends as a joyful and kindhearted woman. She is not defined by the challenges in her life, but rather by the goodness that pours from her life and through her words. Just like Linda, each of us has a choice as to how we will be defined. We often are identified by the words that come out of our mouths—for our words reveal who we really are.

I recently heard a silly story about a little girl who named her dog Aunt Ruth. When she was asked why she chose such a peculiar name, she responded, "I named my dog Aunt Ruth because she's just like my Aunt Ruth. She growls at everyone who passes by and barks constantly about anything that upsets her." Well, now, I'm not sure if I would want to meet the real Aunt Ruth! We certainly are known by what we say and how we say it, aren't we? A whiny woman is not very lovely or appealing.

How would you like people to describe you? I'd much rather be known as kind, joyful, grateful, and encouraging, rather than grumbling, whiny, discouraging, and complaining. Wouldn't you? What comes out of our mouths paints a picture of what is in our hearts. If we are growing in our trust in the Lord, it comes out in our words of hope and contentment no matter what the circumstances. Yet if people hear bitterness, gossip, and frustration pour out of our mouths, we reveal the anger and worry in our hearts.

> *What comes out of our mouths paints a picture of what is in our hearts.*

Just because we have troubles doesn't mean we need to repeat them over and over again to everyone we encounter. There is no rule that states we are required to complain just because our situation has turned bad. And certainly we are not entitled to bad-mouth or gossip about someone because we think he or she deserves it. Our words are important, and we must use our tongues with caution. Our communication can bring life and joy, or it can bring hurt and destruction.

I know there are times when we need to sort things through and talk about them with a helpful friend, mentor, or counselor.

Please don't get me wrong. There is a difference between sharing your situation in order to receive wise counsel and sharing your troubles over and over again in the form of complaining and whining. Let's recognize the difference and remember that pouring out our hearts to God and helpful people can be a positive step toward finding solutions. On the other hand, grumbling brings us down as well as everyone around us.

The Tree of Words

We don't want to be known only for our sorrows and our tragedies, do we? Wouldn't we rather be known as women who have seen God's mighty hand at work? Don't we want to be gracious women who are full of praise for God and encouragement for others? My friend, your challenges or tragedies do not need to define who you are. We can be beautiful, faithful, godly women despite the unexpected twists and turns life brings. Our words reveal our inner beauty based on trusting God, but our words can also reveal our inner ugliness grounded in anger and resentment.

Let's get to the root of the issue: our hearts. Jesus used a tree analogy in quite a pointed conversation with the Pharisees. Here's

> *"A good person produces good things from the treasury of a good heart."—Jesus*

what he said: "A tree is identified by its fruit. If a tree is good, its fruit will be good. If a tree is bad, its fruit will be bad. You brood of snakes! How could evil men like you speak what is good and right? For whatever is in your heart determines what you say. A good person produces good things from the treasury of a good heart, and an evil person produces evil things from the treasury of an evil heart."[1]

Jesus is not leaving a lot of guesswork about our words, is he? Bitter words will come from a bitter heart, just as bitter fruit will come from a bitter tree. The same is true for resentment, anger, and unforgiveness. But on the other hand, if our hearts are filled with joy, contentment, thankfulness, and forgiveness, we will bear lovely fruit as well.

Additional fruit on our tree of words can be exaggeration, dishonesty, or embellishment. As we tell and retell our situation, or someone else's situation for that matter, it is easy for our words to get out of line. Even David, a man after God's own heart, prayed that God would "set a guard over [his] mouth."[2] We can pray a similar prayer: "Lord, help me only say what is good and honest and true. Guard my lips and help them to only reflect your goodness."

Testimonies for Good

How pretty are your feet? Doesn't that seem like an odd question to ask in a chapter about our words? But the Bible uses an illustration about feet to talk about the good message we bring to others. "How beautiful . . . are the feet of those who bring good news!" we read in both Romans and Isaiah.[3] When we bring good news to others about salvation in Jesus, the Bible says we have beautiful feet. And you thought the only way to have beautiful feet was to shop the sale at Nordstrom!

God is very serious about what comes out of our mouths, for his Word tells us that if we confess with our mouths that Jesus is Lord and believe in our hearts that God raised him from the dead, we are saved. "For 'everyone who calls on the name of the LORD will be saved.'"[4] Our mouths are used for confessing our faith in Christ, they are used for bringing the good news of God's love and salvation to others, and they are used for healing and helping others.

Throughout the book of Proverbs we are reminded about the power of our words. Solomon said: "Wise words are like deep waters; wisdom flows from the wise like a bubbling brook."[5] But he also said: "The mouths of fools are their ruin; they trap themselves with their lips."[6]

I've listened to people (and I'm sure you have too) who talk and talk and talk and talk about their problems. They talk about how bad their husbands are or how awful their jobs are or if they wouldn't have done this, or if that hadn't happened. They spend so much time talking about their problems that they don't have an opportunity to look for solutions or consider God's goodness and the hope he brings. The mouth can keep us on a route to destruction, but it can also be a great gift to others.

In the Old Testament, we see that David's life wasn't easy. He continually faced obstacles, death, giants, and enemies of all sorts, yet he saw God's constant provision. He knew that God would not leave him, and he declared it over and over again. He said, "I will praise the LORD at all times. I will constantly speak his praises."[7] Obviously his heart was filled with thanksgiving and praise for God. He focused on God's qualities instead of his own mistakes, fears, and frustrations.

We can look at women throughout history who chose to declare God's goodness instead of grumbling about their circumstances.

Fanny Crosby (1820–1915), blinded at six weeks of age due to improper medical treatment, could have held bitterness and resentment in her heart and allowed it to pour out in her words. Instead, Fanny chose to use her words to bring glory to God and to encourage others in their faith. It is estimated that she wrote more than eight thousand songs in her lifetime. At the age of eight, this positive young woman wrote the following words:

> Oh, what a happy soul am I!
> Although I cannot see,

I am resolved that in this world
Contented I will be.

How many blessings I enjoy
That other people don't!
To weep and sigh because I'm blind,
I cannot, and I won't.

Of course as she grew, her words grew too. I'm sure you are familiar with some of Fanny Crosby's hymns, such as "All the Way My Savior Leads Me," "Blessed Assurance," "Rescue the Perishing," and "Saved by Grace." To this day, Fanny's hymns bring healing and hope to all who worship God through her glorious words.

Fanny's life wasn't marked by her blindness, but by her words of thankfulness and praise to God! Don't you wonder how her family and friends chose the songs to sing at her funeral? I bet it was a pretty long funeral if they sang even a small portion of all the songs she wrote.

Elisabeth Elliot could have chosen words of anger and hostility, especially toward the Auca Indians who killed her husband. She could have lashed out at God, questioning how a sovereign, loving God could allow a faithful missionary and his three companions to be killed in cold blood simply because they were bringing the gospel message to the Auca tribe in Ecuador. But Elisabeth Elliot chose instead to use her words and actions for forgiveness and to bring hope to the very people who had killed her husband.

After her husband's death, Elisabeth and her young daughter, Valerie, decided to stay at their mission station in the jungle in order to further the work her husband had started. Eventually she moved into the village with the Auca people and stayed there for two years, learning their language with the hope that someday the Bible could be translated in their language. Other missionaries and translators helped, and in 1992 the Auca Indians received their own translation of the New Testament.

Elisabeth went on to write a book about her husband's experience, as well as many other inspirational books. Here's what she wrote in her book called *A Path through Suffering*:

> Faith need never ask, "But what good did this do me?" Faith already knows that everything that happens fits into a pattern for good to those who love God. An inconvenience is always, whether we see it or not, a *blessed* inconvenience. We may rest in the promise that God is fitting together a good many more things than are any of our business. We need never see "what good it did," or how a given trouble accomplishes anything. It is peace to leave it all with Him, asking only that He do with me anything He wants anywhere, anytime, that God may be glorified.[8]

Now those are the words of a woman who had eternity in her heart and mind. We may not be able to say what Elisabeth Elliot said, but we can certainly see an example of a woman who has learned to walk in belief rather than bitterness. What a powerful reminder of the truth we find in the book of Romans: "We know that God causes everything to work together for the good of those who love God and are called according to his purpose for them."[9] We all need to be reminded that God fits the unexpected or inconvenient situations in our lives into something good. If Elisabeth Elliot could speak with hope in her situation, perhaps we can begin to speak of hope in ours. Like Fanny Crosby before her, Elisabeth is not remembered for her tragedy, but rather for her victory beyond her tragic loss.

Practically Speaking

How do your words represent you? Do they portray a woman who is walking in faith and trust in God? Or do they represent a fearful, bitter woman who has no hope? We are a testimony to the world of what faith looks like. God continually tells us through his Word, "Fear not, for I am with you."[10] If we believe this is true, then we ought to sound like women who believe God is with us and can be trusted. Hopefully our words sound different from the whining and complaining of those who have no faith.

> *Hopefully our words sound different from the whining and complaining of those who have no faith.*

Since words are an outpouring of our hearts, let's examine your heart condition. I want to end this chapter by giving you some practical ideas to help you develop a deeper, daily hope in the Lord. My desire is for the hope in your heart to grow to the point that it will burst over the top and flow out of your mouth. Consider the following hopeful heart builders.

Daily praise. Take time each morning to praise the Lord for who he is, what he has done, and what he will do. The more we praise the Lord in our own personal time with him, the more it will pour out from our lips in other situations. Praise him for his sovereignty and for his power. Praise him for his ability to make all things work together for good. Praise him for his love, mercy, and care. David found joy in the midst of his challenges as he praised God continually. He said, "I will praise you, LORD, with all my heart; I will tell of all the marvelous things you have done. I will be filled with joy because of you. I will sing praises to your name, O Most High."[11]

Positive Input. We must consider what we allow to impact our way of thinking. If we listen to and get advice from negative or bitter people, then we will have a tendency to lean in that direction. There are also certain books, magazines, or even television shows that can have a negative effect on us, breeding anger, discontentment, or sin. Now, I'm not saying we need to live in a happy bubble, but I am saying we must carefully consider what we put in our minds. Let's be deliberate about consuming positive information. Uplifting books, magazines, and shows, plus encouraging friends can serve to inspire us rather than make us negative people. Most important, we want to fill our hearts and minds with God's Word. The Bible says, "All Scripture is inspired by God and is useful to teach us what is true and to make us realize what is wrong in our lives. It corrects us when we are wrong and teaches us to do what is right. God uses it to prepare and equip his people to do every good work."[12]

Memorize hope-filled scriptures. When you hide God's Word in your heart, it will overflow from your mouth. Choose passages that are meaningful for your situation and will build your trust in God's love and care for you. Recently, I memorized several passages in the Psalms. I have found that the words from these passages pour out of my mouth in conversations with friends and when I need to encourage another person. Certainly they encourage me as well. The psalmist said, "I have hidden your word in my heart, that I might not sin against you."[13]

Pray before complaining. Before a grumble comes out of your mouth, take it to the Lord. Ask the Lord to set a guard over your mouth so your words will refresh and encourage others rather than bring them down. Make this a continual practice in your life. When you feel like complaining, stop and think, *Have I prayed about this yet?* You may want to take a moment to write out your prayer or concerns to God in a journal. He wants to hear our heartfelt cry. Often when we take our concerns and fears to the Lord, we lose the need or desire to whine out loud. Remember, no one likes a whiner, so choose your words wisely. Paul said: "Do everything without complaining and arguing, so that no one can criticize you. Live clean, innocent lives as children of God, shining like bright lights in a world full of crooked and perverse people."[14]

Talk with a trusted friend, mentor, or counselor. As I said earlier, we do need to talk out our problems at times because it helps us sort things through in our minds. Without a doubt, we need counsel and encouragement when we are facing difficult situations. As we share our heartaches with the purpose of moving through the healing process, we take positive steps to finding help and solutions. If we repeat our stories with no desire to get better, then we stay in the pit of despair and grumbling. God wants us to move forward, and often he uses a wise friend or mentor to lead us in a new direction. In Ecclesiastes, we read, "Two people are better off than one, for they can help each other succeed. If one person falls, the other can reach out and help. But someone who falls alone is in real trouble."[15]

Go to sleep each night thanking God. Thank God for his provisions for today and for how he will care again for you tomorrow. As we fill our last thoughts of the day with thankfulness, we end our day with faith-filled thoughts that ruminate in our subconscious minds as we sleep. In the Psalms, we read, "Give thanks to the Lord, for he is good! His faithful love endures forever."[16] In the New Testament, we read Paul's encouragement to have grateful hearts: "Always be joyful. Never stop praying. Be thankful in all circumstances, for this is God's will for you who belong to Christ Jesus."[17]

As we practice these hope builders, our faith and trust in God will most likely spill out into what we do and say. Imagine with me for a moment that you are carrying two mugs in your hand, one filled with hot coffee and one filled with fresh, cool water. As you are carrying them, you stumble and they slosh out and spill on your clothing. You can imagine you aren't too happy with the burn from the coffee as well as the stain that is left behind. Of course the water spill is no problem, and you probably will use some of the water to clean up the coffee stain, right?

Now think about those two liquids as representing the condition of our hearts. The hot coffee represents burning anger and resentment (no offense toward us coffee drinkers!), and the water represents a pure heart of contentment and faith. When life trips us up, the contents of our hearts spill over through our mouths. One burns and stains; the other cleanses. Let's determine to examine our hearts and speak pure and cleansing words that bring life and healing. Anyone can grumble and complain, but few have the faith-filled hope and godly discipline to guard their mouths and tell others what God has done. No matter the circumstances of my life, don't you want my words to be refreshing water to a thirsty soul?

STEPPING FORWARD

 ### POINTS

- What you say identifies who you are.
- Your words are an overflow from your heart.
- Words of gratitude and encouragement bring joy and healing to you and others.
- Words of condemnation and bitterness destroy and hurt both you and others.
- Fill your heart with thankfulness and praise.
- Get rid of discontentment and grumbling.
- Use your words to proclaim what God has done.

 ### PASSAGE: PSALM 71:7–8, 14–21

My life is an example to many,
     because you have been my strength and protection.

That is why I can never stop praising you;
  I declare your glory all day long.

But I will keep on hoping for your help;
  I will praise you more and more.
I will tell everyone about your righteousness.
  All day long I will proclaim your saving power,
  though I am not skilled with words,
I will praise your mighty deeds, O Sovereign LORD.
  I will tell everyone that you alone are just.

O God, you have taught me from my earliest childhood,
  and I constantly tell others about the wonderful
  things you do.
Now that I am old and gray,
  do not abandon me, O God.
Let me proclaim your power to this new generation,
  your mighty miracles to all who come after me.

Your righteousness, O God, reaches to the highest
  heavens.
  You have done such wonderful things.
  Who can compare with you, O God?
You have allowed me to suffer much hardship,
  but you will restore me to life again
  and lift me up from the depths of the earth.
You will restore me to even greater honor
  and comfort me once again.

PRAYER

Marvelous God, I praise you for being my rock and my refuge. You have held me through the storms of life and have set my feet on solid ground. You are able to do great things. Thank you for caring for me and loving me. Thank you for sending your Son, Jesus, to pay the penalty for my sins. Thank you for your Holy Spirit, who will never leave me. Lord, I want to proclaim all you have done in my life. Use my words to glorify you and bless others. Guard my mouth so my words will not be harmful to others. Pour your love through my words to the people around me. In Jesus' name, amen.

PLAN

1. Greet each day with praise to God. You may want to put a sticky note by your alarm clock as a reminder. Write on the note a verse like Psalm 103:1: "Let all that I am praise the LORD; with my whole heart, I will praise his holy name."

2. End each day with thanksgiving to God. Put another reminder sticky note near your toothbrush or on the bathroom mirror. Write verses like Psalm 92:1–2, 4, "It is good to give thanks to the LORD, to sing praise to the Most High. It is good to proclaim your unfailing love in the morning, your faithfulness in the evening. . . . You thrill me, LORD, with all you have done for me!"

3. Tell someone you see today about the wonderful things God is doing in your life.

4. Consider what influences your way of thinking. Get rid of negative influences, and increase positive input.

PART THREE

Live Passionately

If you will call your troubles experiences,
and remember that every experience develops
some latent force within you,
you will grow vigorous and happy,
however adverse your circumstances may seem to be.

John R. Miller

I pray that God, the source of hope,
will fill you completely with joy and peace because you trust in him.
Then you will overflow with confident hope
through the power of the Holy Spirit.

Romans 15:13

Walk boldly and wisely . . .
There is a hand above that will help you on.

Philip James Bailey

9

Your Confident Stride

Taking One Step at a Time in a New Direction

The Sovereign LORD is my strength!
He makes me as surefooted as a deer,
able to tread upon the heights.

Habakkuk 3:19

Anne Beiler began twisting pretzels in 1987 to support her husband Jonas's vision to open a free counseling service in their community. Soon Anne and Jonas purchased their own stand at a farmer's market in Downingtown, Pennsylvania. There was just one problem: the pretzels they sold were awful! After some experimentation with the recipe, the result was a pretzel that Anne and her customers quickly dubbed "better than the best you've ever tasted!"

That was the beginning of Auntie Anne's Soft Pretzels store, which would grow to more than 850 locations in the next seventeen years. Anne's vision was to "give back," so Auntie Anne's has been actively involved in charity, donating millions nationwide. Her biography, *Twist of Faith*, not only tells the story of the building of Auntie Anne's business, but also the tragedies and triumphs of her life.

Anne's journey is a remarkable story of both failure and success. She persevered through a series of difficult personal struggles—including betrayal, depression, and the tragic death of a child. She has become one of the leading female franchise owners in the United States, but she remains open and honest about her struggles.

She says, "Thinking back on my life, the twists and turns it's taken, I feel truly amazed that I am whole. Sometimes even now I cannot believe how high the highs were, or how low the lows—emotionally I went to the very brink of hell and back. . . . Yet somehow I am now thrilled to live this life, feeling that each day is one to be enjoyed. God's grace and forgiveness is what got me through it all."[1]

Anne Beiler knows what it is like to live an unexpected journey of both highs and lows, joys and sorrows. Yet through it all she found a confident stride and a way to make a positive difference in this world.

Like it or not (mostly not), the challenges we face in life make us stronger and wiser as women. Let's be honest, there is not a long line of people waiting to sign up for classes at the school of hard knocks in order to grow to be stronger persons. We don't usually choose our pain. We don't invite it or want it, but it happens, and we must move through it. In the process we grow to be confident, competent women, with pain and hurt sometimes as our best teachers.

> *We grow to be confident, competent women, with pain and hurt sometimes as our best teachers.*

First Steps

Our first steps forward are significant ones. Recently we added a new puppy to our home, and she is no small pup. She's a nine-month-old English mastiff named Bentley. She's sweet, gentle, and loveable, but she is also extremely fearful. It's almost humorous to watch this giant, one-hundred-twenty-pound puppy who is afraid to go through a door or down a step or across a floor. Recently, she bravely followed me upstairs to the second floor of our house. That was all well and good except for the simple fact that she was too frightened to come down the stairs. She just couldn't seem to figure out how to navigate the first step down.

We couldn't allow her to live the rest of her doggy life on the second floor of the house, so I tried to gently help her down. But all she wanted to do was sit there and bark at the steps. After forty-five minutes of coaxing her, I finally got her to take the first step down. (Where is the Dog Whisperer when you need him?) Once Bentley accomplished the first step, the second wasn't too bad. Then the next and the next, and finally she was running free on the first floor again! What a relief for us all! She obviously had the ability to go down the stairs safely; she just didn't have the courage to take that first step.

Bentley's situation made me think how often I nestle safely in my sorrow or resist moving forward because I just don't know how to make the initial move. Sometimes I don't know what to do; and sometimes, out of fear of the unknown, I prefer to just stay put. Instead of taking steps in a positive direction, it is sometimes easier to just sit there and bark (or in human terms, whine and complain). Certainly there are times to be content where God has placed us, but there comes a time when we must take the first step to find our confident stride once again.

For most of us, the first step is typically the hardest one, as well as the most significant. We hesitate to take that first step because we don't know what is down the road. Fear of what the future holds, fear of making a mistake, or fear of living in our new circumstances can stifle us and prevent us from moving forward. Stop for a moment and consider what may be keeping you from moving in a positive direction. You may need to begin with little steps day by day, but the important thing is to not let fear stop you in your tracks.

> *You may need to begin with little steps day by day, but the important thing is to not let fear stop you in your tracks.*

Like a precious toddler, there will be those times when you are walking along and begin to stumble. But just as a parent kindly reaches down and helps the toddler up to his feet, so the Lord is there with you, strengthening you and holding your hand. David put it perfectly when he wrote:

The LORD directs the steps of the godly.
He delights in every detail of their lives.
Though they stumble, they will never fall,
for the LORD holds them by the hand.[2]

My friend, do you see the picture of the Lord's graceful hand helping you up? Keep it in mind as you continue to journey step by step. You may not feel as though you have what it takes, but God can give you the feet you need for the journey ahead. He is strong where you are weak. He is sufficient and able to carry you.

"IT'S NOT ME; IT'S GOD!"

Karen and her husband, John, were finally settled into their new home, where they planned to spend their years of retirement. Karen, a middle-school librarian, and John, an elementary-school principal, were content with their lives and work in Amarillo, Texas.

In December 2006, with their home beautifully decorated for Christmas and presents under the tree, their placid life took a little turn. A fire broke out near the master bedroom. The firemen arrived quickly enough to get the flames under control and prevent the house from incurring too much damage.

Perhaps you have heard that sometimes when a house catches on fire, it can reignite even up to a week after the initial fire. Well, early the next morning at the hotel where they were staying, they received the dreaded phone call. The fire had started back up, and this time it was serious. Jennifer, their daughter, met them at the house to assess the damage. This time the roof was engulfed with flames, and most of the attic was destroyed, causing ceilings to fall and resulting in water and smoke damage throughout. Unbelievable as it sounds, the fire started a third time. It was almost evening, and Karen smelled smoke again. The firemen arrived and extinguished the third fire!

Fortunately, the firefighters were able to save some valued pictures and all the Christmas gifts from under the tree. Karen and John were thankful for the firefighters' noble and brave efforts. God gave Karen one precious reassurance of his help and presence. You see, when she was finally able to trudge through the sludge, she found that miraculously her little prayer room (a converted closet) had been preserved. Her Bible and prayer books came out unscathed. Karen felt as though God had preserved the room as a demonstration of his love and care for them.

As you can imagine, the first few days after a major fire are overwhelming. Responsibilities include cleaning up and sorting through anything that can be salvaged, finding a place to stay, dealing with the insurance, and making decisions for the future. Karen knew she had to step up to the plate and get to work, one decision at a time. Her daughter pitched in to help, and they began progressing forward bit by bit. It was slow and daunting at first, but Karen felt as though she could move forward, knowing that God was with her and leading her every step of the way.

Karen and John were amazed at the outpouring of love and help from family, friends, and neighbors. Strangers drove up and handed them money; others brought food and clothing and gift certificates. As time went on, they were able to rebuild their dream home. Karen and Jennifer even made a fun mother/daughter trip to Oklahoma City one day to buy new furniture for the house. Karen's attitude through the whole process was one of hope and expectancy, with a "What will God do next?" perspective. The family recognized God as their constant companion through the steps they took in order to get back on their feet again.

Karen is a picture of a thriving woman, but she would be the first to tell you, "It's all God, not me." I love Karen's spirit, don't you? Her confident hope was in the Lord and not in herself. We

---

We can't be certain what life will bring, but we can be certain God will be with us.

---

can't be certain what life will bring, but we can be certain God will be with us. Karen's favorite verses are Philippians 4:13, "I can do everything through him who gives me strength" and Romans 8:28, "We know that in all things God works for the good of those who love him, who have been called according to his purpose."

God-Confidence

So where does a girl get confidence—especially when dreams fall apart and she's thrust into an unexpected life? Let's consider what it actually means to have confidence. *Confidence* means to have a firm belief or trust. The root word, *fidere*, is the same root we find in the word *fidelity*, meaning faithful or faith. To have confidence, then, means to have a strong trust or faith in something or someone. Self-confidence is obviously trusting in self. Confidence in people or circumstances can be shaky, but confidence in God puts us on a firm foundation! The Bible reminds us continually that God is a rock and a refuge and worthy of our trust.

Let's explore a few passages from the Bible that specifically talk about confidence:

You have been my hope, O Sovereign LORD, my *confidence* since my youth.[3]—David

Have no fear of sudden disaster or of the ruin that overtakes the wicked, for the LORD will be your *confidence* and will keep your foot from being snared. Do not withhold good from those who deserve it, when it is in your power to act.[4]—Solomon

In the fear of the LORD one has strong *confidence,* and his children will have a refuge. The fear of the LORD is a fountain of life, that one may turn away from the snares of death.[5]—Solomon

Blessed are those who trust in the LORD and have made the LORD their hope and *confidence.*[6]—Jeremiah

Such *confidence* as this is ours through Christ before God. Not that we are competent in ourselves to claim anything for ourselves, but our competence comes from God.[7] —Paul

Each of these passages offers a powerful reminder that we experience confidence when we place our trust in the Lord. God-confidence can help us take that first step forward. God-confidence can help break the chains of fear, which so easily hold us back. When our confidence rests in him, we can walk forward, knowing we are loved and not alone. As Thomas Merton said, "I will not fear, for you are ever with me, and you will never leave me to face my perils alone."[8]

When David fought Goliath, his confidence wasn't in his slingshot and stones; it was in the Lord. When Gideon fought against a vast army, his confidence wasn't in his little army of three hundred men; it was in the Lord. When Esther went before the king to plead for her people, her confidence wasn't in her own power of persuasion; it was in the Lord's power to save her life and the lives of her people. Where does your confidence come from?

Good Posture

Do you have someone in your life who used to harp on you to maintain good posture? "Head up, shoulders back, stomach in, stand straight and tall!" Can't you just hear him or her saying that to

> *True confidence comes from our faith in God's ability to see us through.*

you right now? I bet you just straightened up as you read those commands, didn't you? We all know that good posture makes us look lovely and confident. As important as it is to have good body posture, it is also important for us to have a confident

spiritual posture as we trust God and not ourselves. True confidence comes from our faith in his ability to see us through.

So how do we maintain a confident spiritual posture? Let's look at a few tips to maintaining a good posture spiritually speaking.

Head up. When we turn our focus upward, it takes our eyes off fallible people and faulty circumstances. Our trust is built when we continue to turn our eyes toward the Lord and look expectantly for what he can do and the way he will provide. Turning our thoughts upward demands a conscious decision to stop dwelling on what is wrong in our lives and start looking for what is right. I like how David said, "I am confident I will see the LORD's goodness while I am here in the land of the living. Wait patiently for the LORD. Be brave and courageous. Yes, wait patiently for the LORD."[9] Sometimes turning our eyes upward means waiting in anticipation for what God will do. We may not have all the answers yet, but we can wait in hope as our eyes are fixed on the Lord.

Shoulders back. It's difficult to keep our shoulders back if we are bearing heavy burdens. Instead of hunching over in order to carry a heavy load of worry or guilt, we need to cast our cares upon the Lord. Maybe the heavy load is unforgiveness, and we need to let go of holding something over another person. Maybe the load is guilt or worry or sin. What load are you carrying? Give it over to the Lord, and stand straight and tall with your shoulders free of the heavy weight. When we try to carry our burdens alone, we fall into barely surviving mode. We read in the Psalms, "Give your burdens to the LORD, and he will take care of you. He will not permit the godly to slip and fall." It is only when we release our burdens to him that we begin to truly thrive.

Stomach in. In his letter to the Ephesians, Paul talks about the armor of God and the belt of truth we should wear around our waists. It is easy for us to get distracted with assumptions and speculations that can send our minds into second guessing. We must tighten our muscles and cinch the truth belt at the center of our being—holding on to the truth of what we know about God and his abiding love for us. Feelings can often sway us and lead us into frustration, fear, and sin. Solomon said, "Let not mercy and truth forsake you; bind them around your neck, write them on the tablet of your heart, and so find favor and high esteem in the sight of God and man."[10]

Stand straight and tall. When we stand on God's Word, we will never fall, for it is a sure foundation. We find truth and light, hope and encouragement in the pages of God's Word. When we read God's Word and do what it says, we build our lives on a rock. I am reminded of the illustration

> *It is only when we release our burdens to him that we begin to truly thrive*
> *—Psalm 55:22*

Jesus used of the wise man who built his house on the rock. "Anyone who listens to my teaching and follows it is wise, like a person who builds a house on solid rock. Though the rain comes in torrents and the floodwaters rise and the winds beat against that house, it won't collapse because it is built on bedrock. But anyone who hears my teaching and doesn't obey it is foolish, like a person who builds a house on sand. When the rains and floods come and the winds beat against that house, it will collapse with a mighty crash."[11]

Walk with confidence. Once we have a confident spirit, it is time to step forward in that confidence, putting one foot in front of another. We can take a tip from the apostle Paul, who faced challenges every day as he shared the truth of the gospel. How did he walk with confidence? He knew that this earth wasn't the end of the road and that his body would one day fade away. His goal was to please God and not man. He knew his real home was in heaven, and this knowledge gave him the ability to confidently step forward in faith.

Here's how he put it:

We are always confident, even though we know that as long as we live in these bodies we are not at home with the Lord. For we live by believing and not by seeing. Yes, we are fully confident, and we would rather be away from these earthly bodies, for then we will be at home with the Lord. So whether we are here in this body or away from this body, our goal is to please him. For we must all stand before Christ to be judged. We will each receive whatever we deserve for the good or evil we have done in this earthly body.[12]

Will we allow our disappointments to crush us or compel us to move forward? Business entrepreneur Mary Kay once said, "For every failure, there's an alternative course of action. You just have to find it. When you come to a roadblock, take a detour."[13] The detours of our lives may be unexpected, exciting, or frustrating, but as we start the journey, we can have confidence we are not alone. God is with us as our very present help in time of trouble.[14]

STEPPING FORWARD

POINTS

- Although we would never choose to have difficulties in our lives, we can still grow through them and become stronger and more confident women.
- The first step is usually the hardest and the most significant one.
- Confidence comes from placing our trust in God, not people or circumstances.
- A confident spiritual posture is more important than physical posture:

    Head up—keep your eyes on the Lord.

    Shoulders back—cast your cares continually on the Lord.

    Stomach in—stay centered on truth, not assumptions.

    Stand straight and tall—stand on the sure foundation of hearing and doing God's Word.

    Walk with confidence—walk confidently with eternal perspective

PASSAGE: PSALM 86:1–13

Bend down, O LORD, and hear my prayer;
>answer me, for I need your help.
Protect me, for I am devoted to you.
>Save me, for I serve you and trust you.
>You are my God.
Be merciful to me, O Lord,
>for I am calling on you constantly.

Give me happiness, O Lord,
     for I give myself to you.
O Lord, you are so good, so ready to forgive,
     so full of unfailing love for all who ask for your help.
Listen closely to my prayer, O Lord;
     hear my urgent cry.
I will call to you whenever I'm in trouble,
     and you will answer me.

No pagan god is like you, O Lord.
     None can do what you do!
All the nations you made
     will come and bow before you, Lord;
     they will praise your holy name.
For you are great and perform wonderful deeds.
     You alone are God.
Teach me your ways, O Lord,
     that I may live according to your truth!
Grant me purity of heart,
     so that I may honor you.
With all my heart I will praise you, O Lord my God.
     I will give glory to your name forever,
for your love for me is very great.
     You have rescued me from the depths of death.

 PRAYER

Great and mighty Father, you are the High King of heaven
and the lover of my soul. You are sufficient for my pain and
struggles. I look to you for hope and confidence. Thank
you that you can be trusted. Thank you for your continual
love and kindness. Thank you for never leaving me. Lord, I
ask that you would show me which steps to take. Direct my

path. Give me the strength and courage to step forward. Lead me and help me day by day. In Jesus' name, amen.

PLAN

Take some time to be alone with God. On a big blank sheet of paper (I like to use an artist's sketch pad), write Jeremiah 29:11 at the top.

> "I know the plans I have for you," says the LORD.
> "They are plans for good and not for disaster,
> to give you a future and a hope."

Read the verse several times aloud and prayerfully ask God to give you confidence for your next steps. Draw a picture or write out all the thoughts he brings to mind and shows you. Use this method of prayer and listening whenever you need to make a decision or work toward a new plan. Finally, do a spiritual posture self-check.

- Are you looking up to God in faith, or are you looking only at your circumstances?
- Are you carrying a weight on your shoulders that you should not bear?
- Is truth at the center of your life?
- Are you standing firm on the Word of God?
- Are you walking with confidence?

*No medicine is more valuable, none more efficacious,
none better suited to the cure of all our temporal ills
than a friend to whom we may turn for consolation
in time of trouble, and with whom we may share
our happiness in time of joy.*

Saint Ailred of Rievaulx

10

Healthy Connections

Building Positive Relationships into Your Circle

*As iron sharpens iron,
so a friend sharpens a friend.*

Proverbs 27:17

Sandra Nichols had a wonderful husband and two tremendous sons, but in her heart of hearts she wanted a daughter. She asked God, "If there will be a place eighteen years from now where you could use a godly young woman, would you please give me the opportunity to raise her?" In December of that same year, God gave Sandra and her husband that precious little girl. They named her Natalie.

As her children grew, Sandra prayed for their futures. Little did she know where God's plan would take them. Natalie had a passion for God and a desire to be used by him. At fifteen, she began singing in churches, evangelistic crusades, and state prisons. She was homeschooled and entered college just days after her sixteenth birthday.

At eighteen, she had been accepted as a junior at Baylor University. There she remained an honor student in the top 5 percent of her class, and she diligently pursued her dream of becoming a professional musician. She was offered scholarships for graduate studies at home and abroad. Her participation in the Miss Texas Pageant provided a training ground of which she intended to take advantage. Every day she awoke with excitement, filled with anticipation of the opportunities for performing and for witnessing. She was on top of her world!

However, Natalie's life began to change dramatically. In a matter of weeks, an undiagnosed illness progressed, taking her on a downward spiral. Natalie's life had largely revolved around developing and mastering her talent and skill as a pianist. But her hands and forearms had become stiff and painful. She was no longer able to play the piano. Soon she became unable to attend college as the decline of her health continued.

Finally, in 1996, after eight years of increasing illness, a correct diagnosis was made—late-stage Lyme disease, a disease that over time disseminates more deeply throughout the body if not accurately diagnosed and aggressively treated. By this time, there was little left that resembled the eighteen-year-old who had begun this journey. What began with a flu, fatigue, stiffness, and pain had progressed until Natalie was confined to a wheelchair, then confined to bed. She was unable to feed herself, speak above a whisper, turn her head, or get words and images into her mind. Lyme disease had ravaged her physical health, cognitive skills, personality, and emotional health.

In order to care for Natalie during the years of her severe illness, Sandra had to give up the Christian preschool and childcare center she had owned and operated for more than thirteen years. Sandra's personal faith and expectation in God's faithfulness was tested, but she continued to hold onto the Lord. Natalie's faith was bolstered by her mother's unwavering confidence in the God who is faithful to keeping all his promises.

Only the grace of God sustained Natalie through those years. His grace and his written Word assured her that he loved her; that he, and he alone, is in control; and that all things work together for the good of those who love him. Through God's Word and a personal, intimate relationship with Jesus Christ, Natalie has been infused with his comfort, his peace, his strength, and his eternal perspective.

God is continuing to restore Natalie's health as she receives aggressive medical treatment. Both Sandra and Natalie share the story of God's grace in their lives through speaking and writing. Their story is one of healing and hope as they work together as mother and daughter to bring honor to God.

Sandra and Natalie have been through a difficult journey together. Just as Natalie was a gift from God to Sandra many years ago, Sandra has also been God's gift to Natalie in caring for her through her illness and bolstering her faith along the way. Now Sandra and Natalie minister to others through speaking, writing, and counseling. Their website, Shadesofgrace.org, is evidence of lives that do way more than survive—these women *thrive*. Natalie and Sandra are a source of hope and encouragement to anyone who has faced adversity or just needs a glimpse of God's glory.

God's Provision through People

When our lives takes detours, we must open our eyes and recognize the gift of people God has placed around us. Sometimes we are consumed in our struggle or living in an overwhelmed state and don't see the blessing of the people God has provided. Now, let's be honest and recognize that the people God gives us may be far from perfect. Some are delightful, but others are very different from us, and some may even annoy us at times. Yet God uses all types of people as vessels of his provision to help us through difficult times.

In this chapter we're talking about the blessings of *healthy* connections, but we need to take a moment to acknowledge that not all connections are healthy. It's important to discern the difference between healthy and unhealthy and make wise choices regarding our relationships with people who tend to pull us away from God and doing what is right. That being said, let's turn our attention back to accepting the gifts that come through others. Oddly, when we are drowning, we sometimes have a tendency to push people away instead of allowing them into our world. I'm reminded of years ago when I trained to be a lifeguard. We learned that one of the most dangerous types of rescue is when the victim

God uses all types of people as vessels of his provision to help us through difficult times.

is thrashing and panicking. When that happens, the lifeguard may even be pulled under by the victim. The victim unwittingly keeps at bay his or her own rescue by continuing to kick and scream and trying to make it alone. It is when the drowning person allows the lifeguard to approach that he or she can be saved. Similarly, in the midst of what feels like drowning in our own life circumstances, we may struggle and thrash and tell everyone, "I'm okay, I can do this on my own." But the truth is, we've been created as relational beings. When we are hurting, we must allow people to help us and thus experience God's rescue through their loving hands.

What healthy connections has God provided in your life right now? Whether you have allowed them to help you yet or not, I want you to write their names below.

People God Has Sent into My Life to Help Me:

Take a moment to go back through the names and thank God for each of them and their presence in your life. Be honest with yourself, now; are you allowing these people to get close enough to help? Perhaps you are still trying to swim out of the riptide on your own. It is time to recognize God's loving hand through the touch of these people. Again, they may not necessarily be people you adore or love to be around, but they are people

God has placed in your life to help you and offer some sort of care for you. God can use friends to provide advice as well as practical help. My friend Carrie found herself in a predicament several years ago.

Carrie grew up in a business-minded family with high expectations. She had always pictured herself in the corporate world, and that was exactly where she ended up. Straight out of college, she nabbed her dream job at a major corporation and began working her way up the corporate ladder. She loved the security of a nice income, a corporate car, and a generous expense account. Life was going just as she planned as she settled into a happy life in a big city in the Midwest. That is, until the day Carrie's boss called her into his office and told her she had three days to make a decision whether she would accept a promotion and move to Chicago. Carrie knew that if she didn't take the offer, her career with the big corporation was over. The company expectation was when you are offered a promotion, you either take it or you are finished with the corporate climb.

Carrie had a major decision to make. Not only would she be leaving the life she loved in the Midwest, but she would also be distancing herself from her soon-to-be fiancé, John, who was working on his master's degree at the time. It would mean they would be apart for several years, and she would still be at the mercy of the corporation's possibly sending her to yet another location. Carrie agonized over her decision and felt like she was all alone. She didn't know anyone who had been through a similar situation, and she desperately needed help and advice. Carrie prayed diligently for the next forty-eight hours, seeking the Lord's guidance and direction. God answered her prayer by bringing a helpful friend, Kelly, whose listening ear and timely wisdom helped set Carrie in the right direction.

Kelly encouraged Carrie to write out the pros and cons of moving to Chicago on a legal pad, in order to get every aspect of her decision out of her mind and onto paper. Sometimes our challenges look different

165

in black and white instead of swirling all around in our heads. For Carrie, it was like a light went on when she wrote down the pros and cons. She realized without a doubt she needed to say no to the corporate invitation and step forward in faith to the new place God was leading her.

At first Carrie felt like she was taking a step backward as she moved back to her hometown and moved in with her parents, working as an assistant in a business office. After John and Carrie married, he began pursuing his doctorate, which led him to a small town in Louisiana, not Carrie's dream location by any means. Carrie and John only knew one person in this small town, a friend of Carrie's mom. But sometimes it just takes one person to connect you to the right group of people. This wonderful lady introduced Carrie and John to a church where Carrie met the CEO of a major business. And you guessed it! Carrie took a job with one of the most successful businesses in the area.

After his doctorate was complete in Louisiana, John was offered a dream job in a small town up north close to his family. Carrie always saw herself living in a big, cosmopolitan city, so this was not the life she dreamed she would live. Fortunately, Carrie was able to maintain her work from her new location and has become the sales director for the major accounts in her company. Carrie recently had a baby girl and recognizes she is in the perfect situation to raise a family with her in-laws close by. She is more than grateful for the people God has placed in her life all along the way to guide her and assist her. Carrie is strong, independent, and capable of accomplishing almost anything on her own, but she has learned to love and appreciate what God wants to do through the connections in her life.

Family Blessing

One of the most significant connections in our lives is family. Family members can be there for us not only in happy times and celebrations, but they can also step in during the tough times if we will let them.

Mary Sue has been married to Jack for more than fifty years. Jack was always a vibrant and healthy man until he experienced a debilitating stroke several years ago. It was a shock to his family as well as all who knew him through business. Even in his seventies, Jack was still quite busy in his career as a life insurance consultant traveling all over the world. When the stroke occurred, the entire family surrounded Mary Sue to offer support.

Mary Sue is a lovely example of a wise woman who recognizes God's provision. Instead of trying to bear the burden of Jack's care on her own, she graciously received the help God provided right in her midst.

Jack's brother Garry came alongside Mary Sue to help her in the decision for Jack's care. When Jack was first in the hospital, Garry created a schedule for each of the family members to sit with him so he wasn't alone. It was an amazing picture of coming together. Family and friends have continued to offer support, and Mary Sue has graciously received the help she needs to carry on for the journey ahead. Her uplifting attitude and positive perseverance have been a powerful example. Mary Sue is a courageous and strong woman who has the wisdom to allow others to help. As Solomon said, "Friends love through all kinds of weather, and families stick together in all kinds of trouble."[1]

Mary Sue's story is significant to me personally because Mary Sue is my aunt, and Garry is my dad. I'm grateful for the example both Mary Sue and my dad set for the rest of the family. Through this experience, we've bonded closer together as a family and learned what it means to be there for one another in time of need.

Blessed Lifelines through Friendships

Family is typically the first line of support when our lives take a difficult turn, but many people don't have that luxury. Either family members are too far away, not able to help, or sadly, some may not be willing to help. There are times when we may need friends to step in and take the place family members normally would. Some friends may have been your friends even before the adversity, but sometimes friendships are born through adversity.

Let's take a look at a couple of ways you can build a bridge of connection in your time of need. First, consider the groups in which you are currently involved. Don't just assume they know about your situation or are aware of your needs. As much as we would love for people to step up to the plate and jump right in and help, it doesn't always happen. In today's world, many people are busy and wrapped up in their own lives. Everyone could use a little heads-up to know how to help. So if you are in a Sunday-school class or a small group from your church or a MOPS group or a Bible study, I want to encourage you to call some in the group and tell them your prayer needs as well as your immediate practical needs.

> *Don't just assume that others know about your situation or are aware of your needs.*

I've learned that although most people are busy, they really do want to help. Giving an indication of your needs (without high expectations attached) can help people know how to lend a hand. I know, I know, we are told to always just step in and help those in need. But often people cannot step up and help you if they don't know you have a need. We want to be careful not to come across as "needy" all the time, but there is a careful balance of allowing people to help when you need it without asking for too much.

If you don't have a support group, it may be time to seek one out. A quick search on the internet will help you discover a particular type of local support group that could help you. Here are a few support groups that may fit your needs.

Crown Ministries (financial counseling)—www.crown.org
Cancer support—www.mdanderson.org/patients_public/
   support_programs/

Alcoholics Anonymous—www.aa.org

Grief Recovery—www.griefshare.org

Children with Disabilities—www.joniandfriends.org

Divorce Recovery—www.divorcecare.org

Divorce Recovery for kids—www.dc4k.org

Celebrate Recovery—www.celebraterecovery.com

Caregivers support—www.caregiver.com

Supportive friends can emerge from one of these groups, but friends may come from many other sources as well. Keep your heart and mind open to the people God puts in your pathway. You may make a friend at the hospital or in the doctor's waiting room or at physical therapy. The person in the cubicle next to yours may need a kind word, or the mom next door may need a hug. Don't just talk about your needs; find out about theirs. Reach out in the place you are at right now. You may think you don't have the energy or time to make a new friend, but if you will use the opportunities in your new situation to build a connection, you will experience the joy of budding friendships.

Take a genuine interest in others, and they will take an interest in you. Be an encouragement to others, and you will find yourself encouraged as well. Love someone who is unlovely and difficult to love, and you may break through the wall around her heart and find a new friend.

> *Take a genuine interest in others, and they will take an interest in you.*

While you are looking for a friend, be a friend. The result will be a heart filled with joy as you have lifted another person up. If we take the first step to touch another person's life, we may be surprised at the connection that follows. Solomon reminds us, "A real friend sticks closer than a brother."[2] Let's seek to be a real friend through caring for others, for as we do, we will find we are cared for as well.

KEEPING THE MARRIAGE STRONG THROUGH TOUGH TIMES

As a girl, Kim pictured herself in a fairy-tale marriage living "happily ever after," but that's not exactly how her marriage with Richard turned out. In fact, Kim and Richard were married, then divorced, then remarried to each other again, then separated, then back together again. In some ways their marriage has been more like a roller coaster than a fairy tale, yet now their marriage is a testimony of God's love and hope.

Kim will be the first to tell you that as a young married couple they lived wild and selfish lives. They pointed fingers in blame, drew a few lines in the sand, and expected the other person to do the changing to meet their needs. Both Richard and Kim admit there was a bit of pride on both parts (who among us hasn't been there?), but through the help of loving friends they were able to come to a place of reconciliation twice. God began to work in Kim's and Richard's hearts, helping them embrace the fact that their marriage was a lifelong commitment.

Learning to die to self has enabled them to come together and move forward. Now Richard and Kim are madly in love with each other. She said it's almost like the giddy honeymoon stage, only better. They have truly learned to love in a Christlike way, thinking of the other rather than simply living for self. Kim says she tells married couples two things from what they have learned from their own experience: die to self and never lose hope. She said, "Just when you are going around a difficult bend, have hope; there could be a whole beautiful picture around the next corner." One of Kim's favorite Bible verses is, "Now to him who is able to do immeasurably more than all we ask or imagine, according to his power that is at work within us."[3]

Richard and Kim's story is a reminder to us all of the importance of keeping our marriages strong and the joy of truly loving each other. Their story is also a reminder that we need God's help and guidance to live selfless lives. Dying to self doesn't come naturally; rather it comes supernaturally from a God who self-lessly sent his Son to die on our behalf. In order to thrive, mar-riages need continual maintenance, especially during the tough and unexpected turns of life. With his strength and direction, we can find a hope beyond what we could ever ask or imagine. God can resurrect a love between you and your spouse, even when you think the relationship is dead and gone.

Keeping a marriage strong during normal times is difficult, but when challenges or even tragedy strikes, it can seem impossible. But you and your husband need to function as a team and join forces for support rather than working against each other—especially during the tough times. Here are some marriage dos and don'ts to keep in mind in the midst of troubling circumstances.

> *In order to thrive, marriages need continual maintenance, especially during the tough and unexpected turns of life.*

Do stay connected through communication. Often we make as-sumptions about what the other person is thinking or doing. Talk together about expectations, desires, and details. Share your fears, concerns, and hopes as well. Don't assume your husband knows how you feel or understands what you are going through.

Do accept your differences. As you and your husband cope with stress or loss, recognize that you may handle the situation and grief differently from each other. Appreciate the differences; don't let them annoy you.

Do speak lovingly and respectfully to each other. Build up your hus-band with your words and with your tone. You are both struggling and need encouragement. Give, and it will be given back to you. If you give anger and disrespect, guess what you will receive?

Do set aside a regular time to talk with each other. A regular date night would be tremendous, if possible. Schedule a face-to-face visit—and you don't always have to talk about your problems. Sharing other parts of your lives can refresh your relationship. Laugh together; it's good medicine.

Do start praying together each night. As you and your husband go together before the Lord, you begin to bond in a deeper way spiritually, but you also are giving your cares to God. Together you begin to recognize that the solutions are not all in your hands. The final result rests in God's.

Do stay flexible. You and your husband may see the situation from different angles. Be open to his opinion, and kindly ask him to be open to yours. Encourage each other to consider the other's perspective and viewpoint. God has put you together as a team, and each of you brings unique gifts and perceptions to the table. Be willing to let go of your way as the only way. Oddly, sometimes our husbands may be right. Imagine that!

Do seek counseling if you need it. If you notice that you and your husband are starting to work against each other or are drifting apart, a biblically based counselor or pastor from your church can help you sort through some of the issues. Perhaps you could visit with another couple who has been through a similar situation. If you sense you need counseling and your husband won't go, then go by yourself just to help you get a fresh perspective and advice.

Here are a few areas to steer clear of in your marriage:

Don't keep score. Let me tell you right now, if you're keeping score, most likely your husband will never do enough. And he may be thinking the same about you if he is keeping score. Yes, each of you has separate responsibilities, but don't keep a mental balance sheet. Give without expectations. You both can't always live up to the other's standard, so stop playing the Even Steven game.

Don't expect your husband to meet your emotional needs. Keep your prayer life strong and turn to God with your emotional needs. A good friend, a journal, or a counselor can all help with the emotions you are feeling. Remember, your husband is not equipped and was not born to fill your emotional void. Ultimately, only God can heal your emotional wounds.

Don't harbor unforgiveness or bitterness. It's time to release the right to hold something over your husband. Remember, forgiveness doesn't mean you are going to allow him to do whatever he did again. Set healthy boundaries. We've already talked about forgiveness in chapter 6, so you may want to review it again. In obedience to God, we must forgive.

> *Your husband is not equipped and was not born to fill your emotional void.*

Don't shout, scream, accuse, blame, or degrade your husband. Take the high ground and lovingly communicate with your husband in order to work out the issues you are facing. Shouting, screaming, and degrading your husband, especially in front of the kids, are quite unbecoming actions for a woman.

Whether you are married or not, these dos and don'ts can help you in relating to the friends and family around you who are offering you support. Review these principles often as they will serve you well in relating to others through the bad times and the good. If you are going through a difficult time, the last thing you want is for the important relationships in your life to falter. For better or for worse, you need the support of others.

A Humble Thought

We are never so much like a two-year-old as when we have the attitude, "I can do it myself!" Yes, those little tough toddlers try to express their independence by demanding their own way or trying to prove they can accomplish everything on their own. But part of the maturing and thriving process is learning we can't do it all on our own. God provides other people to counsel us, advise us, and help us. We really do need one another; and ultimately, we all need the Lord.

Jill Rigby, author of *Raising Respectful Children in a Disrespectful World*, tells the story of when she hit an all-time unexpected low in her life. After twenty years of marriage, her husband walked into the house one day and told her he was leaving. Her twin boys were only twelve years old at the time. Jill says she hit rock bottom, unable to function on her own. Her mother moved in to help her with the boys and run the household. Jill remembers at the lowest moment, her mother literally helped her in the shower and washed her hair for her—she even brushed Jill's teeth.

Jill had been a Christian since she was seven, but she had never experienced a major crisis in her life and certainly never thought she would be divorced. All the dreams she had for her life suddenly vanished when her husband walked out the door. She was almost numb and couldn't feel God's presence. Her mother was a gift from God to help her with her basic needs, but one day remains in Jill's memory as the turning point in her struggle. Her mother had left the house for a short while. Jill walked into her kitchen on a cold November morning, and the sun was pouring through the window. It hit her face and warmed her whole body. She had always likened the warmth from the sun to the warmth the Holy Spirit brings to our lives. Now in a very real way, she was feeling God's love.

Jill began to move forward that day as she prayed to God for help. She even went so far as to tell God, "I can't help you help me. I'm done. It's yours." God became her strength to carry on, and she recognized she could do nothing without him. When her mother returned to the house and saw Jill up and blow-drying her hair, she looked into her face and knew the old Jill had returned. They held each other and cried and cried. God was healing Jill's heart. Her mother was a tangible gift from God, given to help her through the process.

Jill's story offers a picture of the healing power of our Lord and also the precious gift he gives us in other people. Ultimately, people can't heal our deepest wounds; only God can. Yet the people God places in our lives can be the salve we need in the healing process. Don't push others away through your pain; invite them into your circle. They can pray for you, counsel you, and simply be there to hug you.

STEPPING FORWARD

 ### POINTS

- God uses the people in our lives to help us and give us support.
- Don't push away the people God brings. Listen to their advice and allow support.
- Make new connections by sincerely caring about others.
- Build on the relationships that emerge from support groups and with others who are going through similar challenges.
- Keep your marriage strong through healthy communication.
- While ultimately our healing comes from God, friends can be a salve to help the healing process.

 ### PASSAGE: ROMANS 12:9–16

Don't just pretend to love others. Really love them. Hate what is wrong. Hold tightly to what is good. Love each other with genuine affection, and take delight in honoring each other. Never be lazy, but work hard and serve the Lord enthusiastically. Rejoice in our confident hope. Be patient in trouble, and keep on praying. When God's people are in need, be ready to help them. Always be eager to practice hospitality.

Bless those who persecute you. Don't curse them; pray that God will bless them. Be happy with those who are happy, and weep with those who weep. Live in harmony with each other. Don't be too proud to enjoy the company of ordinary people. And don't think you know it all!

 ## PRAYER

Loving and faithful Father, I praise you, for you will never leave me. Thank you for being the perfect friend. Thank you for healing my wounded heart. Thank you for the people you have sent into my life. Help me stay connected to them. Please strengthen my relationships and teach me to be a good friend to others. Open my eyes to new relationships ready to be formed and give me the grace to make lasting connections with others. In Jesus' name, amen.

 ## PLAN

1. Write a note or email to someone (family or friend) who has been a support to you, and thank that person for being a part of God's healing hand in your life. Tell your friend several qualities you appreciate about him or her, and be sure to include a sincere dose of hearty encouragement.
2. If you are married, take a moment today to tell your husband that you love him and appreciate him.
3. Make a point this week to intentionally pray about your relationships, asking the Lord to strengthen current relationships and open your eyes to new ones.

*The true way to soften one's troubles
is to solace those of others.*

Madame de Maintenon

11

Life Is Not a Spectator Sport

Using Your God-Given Abilities to Be a Blessing to This World

Give, and you will receive. Your gift will return to you in full—pressed down, shaken together to make room for more, running over, and poured into your lap. The amount you give will determine the amount you get back.

Luke 6:38

When Beth's son, Kurt, was born with Goldenhar syndrome, she immediately knew her life was going to go along a new and different path than the one she originally thought it would. Goldenhar syndrome includes an array of different anomalies for the child, primarily craniofacial. Beth would tell you it has been a beautiful journey as well as a challenging one. Through Kurt's eighteen surgeries, Beth met many struggling parents going through similar challenges. The parents felt a special connectedness. Beth became a helpful support to the other parents, while Kurt became an encouragement to thousands of young people.

When Kurt was seven years old, he was invited to play a character on the popular children's show *Barney & Friends*. Because of Kurt's own hearing disability, he played the role of "Jason," a hearing-impaired child on the show. Kurt brought hope to many kids with challenges. Ninety percent of his fan mail came from children with disabilities. Kids who wouldn't wear their hearing aids saw Kurt wearing his and decided to put their own on. Now Kurt (twenty-three years old) is planning to work in the medical industry. He has served others on the mission field in the Dominican Republic and Mexico, and he would love to one day use his medical skills in mission work as well. Kurt knows what it is like to receive help and now loves to return the favor.

We don't want to waste our pain, and one of the ways we can use it is to be an encouragement or support to others. God can use each and every disappointment in our lives as an appointment to lift up another person. There is no greater joy than knowing you are using your experience or even your pain to bring help and hope to another person.

> *We don't want to waste our pain, and one of the ways we can use it is to be an encouragement to others.*

One of the best ways to get out of our own ruts is to help others out of theirs. We can learn the joy that comes from reaching out to others at any age. Here's an idea from my friend Jennifer, who used something as simple as a birthday party as an opportunity to help others:

Jen was ready to do something different for her daughter's sixth birthday party. Her daughter didn't need more toys to add to all the toys she already had, so Jen came up with an idea to not only celebrate her daughter's birthday, but to teach the kids compassion in a very special way. She went to one of the local dollar stores with her camera and took pictures of a variety of different items. I'm sure the employees must have thought Jen was a little bizarre!

Jen went home, printed out the pictures, and glued them on separate index cards. All the kids were invited to bring five dollars with them instead of a present. When they arrived at the party, they went to the Dollar Store and had a scavenger hunt. That's right. They were given five pictures of items to find, and these precious little partygoers scooted around the store searching for their items. This was probably a first for the Dollar Store. Not many people choose to have their parties there. The kids gleefully searched for their items and paid for them.

Next on the party agenda was the local children's home. Jen had already called ahead to find out what kind of toys the children would want, and she scheduled a time to bring the gifts. The party kids had a blast, bringing in the toys from the Dollar Store and giving them to the girls at the children's home. The party was a great success! The kids at the home received love and sweet gifts, and the party kids experienced the joy that comes from caring about others.

Compassion Comes from the Lord

Jesus was the perfect picture of compassion. He reached out to the sick, the lame, the blind, the hurting, and the wounded; and he encouraged his followers to do the same. He taught us to look beyond our own needs and see the needs of others. Jesus gave us a picture of what it means to truly love others through the illustration of the Good Samaritan. Here's the story:

> A Jewish man was traveling on a trip from Jerusalem to Jericho, and he was attacked by bandits. They stripped him of his clothes, beat him up, and left him half dead beside the road.
>
> By chance a priest came along. But when he saw the man lying there, he crossed to the other side of the road and passed him by. A Temple assistant walked over and looked at him lying there, but he also passed by on the other side.
>
> Then a despised Samaritan came along, and when he saw the man, he felt compassion for him. Going over to him, the Samaritan soothed his wounds with olive oil

and wine and bandaged them. Then he put the man on his own donkey and took him to an inn, where he took care of him. The next day he handed the innkeeper two silver coins, telling him, "Take care of this man. If his bill runs higher than this, I'll pay you the next time I'm here."[1]

In this picture of compassion, Jesus teaches us what dying to self really looks like. I think one of the reasons this story touches my heart is because this Samaritan was not reaching out to help a friend, or even someone who liked him. He was helping a man from a culture that despised him. When is the last time you stepped out to help someone who didn't like you? To be quite honest, it is difficult for me sometimes to go the extra mile for people who like me, much less my enemies. But here is the Samaritan who gave of his love, his care, his time, and his money. I believe this kind of compassion is a God-size compassion.

The Bible tells us God is "compassionate and gracious, slow to anger and abounding in love."[2] If we want to see the ultimate picture of compassion, we can look to Jesus himself, who not only cared for his enemies but died for them. If we're honest with ourselves, generally speaking, each of us tends toward selfishness. The good news is we can go to a compassionate God and ask him to open our eyes to the needs around us. He has equipped each one of us with ways we can bless other people. Often it is through our pain and struggles that we gain the wisdom and experience to help others.

Let's choose to be like the Good Samaritan, who had a heart of compassion and gave of his time and resources to touch another life. Instead of walking away from the hurting one, he walked toward him and soothed his wounds with what he had. May the Lord open our eyes to the needs around us. There are people we can soothe with encouraging words because we have been there before. There are others we can bless by giving our time or our money. Lord, lead us down your road of compassion.

Wilted Flowers—Wonderful Opportunity

Edna Ellison is an author and speaker who lives in Spartanburg, South Carolina. She tells the story of how God brought beauty out of a challenging situation. Not only did God give her a special miracle for her daughter's wedding, but she was able to bless someone else's life in the process. I'll let her tell the story:

MAGNOLIA MIRACLE
By Edna Ellison

"Here I am! I stand at the door and knock."
—Revelation 3:20 NIV

It began as an extraordinary weekend. My only daughter, Patsy, was getting married on Saturday, June 17, 1989. I had worked for months to see that all details were in place: making many visits to our local florist for bride's and bridesmaids' bouquets, groomsmen's boutonnieres, and church sanctuary decorations, and then to a different florist for decorations for a reception hall in Newberry, 30 miles away, where Patsy and her fiancé, Tim, were going to be married. The church was across the street from her new home—and down the road from the site of her first full-time job. My florist suggested I could save money by borrowing flowers from my friends and taking them to Newberry. I knew many friends who had lush magnolia blossoms in bloom, so I arranged to pick up a carload of magnolias the night before the wedding. Tim and Patsy offered to help me place them at the front of the sanctuary.

Walking the bride down the aisle was no problem. My son, Jack, offered to do that, since his father had died about five years before. He teased Patsy and said he'd wanted to give her away since she was about three.

Tim's aunt wanted to bake the wedding cake, and I feared it might be covered with plastic columns or a cheap bride-and-groom figurine that would topple over in the middle of the reception. Then she told me she would place white rosebuds on the layers, and I had a new fear: ants or other insects would climb out and walk on the cake just as we sliced it for guests! (I shouldn't have worried; it was delicious, and I later learned that she is a master chef!)

I also worried about the chocolate groom's cake, Patsy's dress, the spelling on the engraved napkins, the reception chefs white hat, the way he carved the roast, the ice for punch, the minister's on-time arrival, and all the other little details of the day.

The night before the wedding, Tim's parents provided a wonderful rehearsal dinner, and afterwards Patsy, Tim, and I banked the choir loft in the sanctuary with beautiful magnolias. When we left that night, the sanctuary was a wonderland of large white flowers and slick green leaves. Before we left, we set the air conditioner on a low temperature so the flowers would be fresh overnight.

The next day, while Patsy dressed, Tim and I went to check on the flowers. As we opened the sanctuary door, a gust of hot air hit us. (We found out later that an evening electrical storm had knocked out the air conditioner.) To my surprise, all the flowers were black! Funeral-black, dead flowers!

Tim asked me to go out into the community to get more magnolias and he'd help me place them as soon as he put his cummerbund on his tuxedo. I left quickly, jumping into my car, searching for white magnolias. I could see trees in the distance with white tops. I stopped before the trees with beautiful magnolias. I prayed for three things: safety across the yard (without a vicious dog that might emerge from the bushes and bite my leg), a nice person who would answer the door, and a willing magnolia donor without a shotgun when I asked to rip his tree to shreds!

The older man who came to the door seemed nice enough. No shotgun. No dog. He climbed a stepladder and handed me armloads of magnolia boughs. As I placed the last bunch in my car, I said, "Sir, you have made the mother of a bride very happy."

He said, "No. You don't understand what's going on, do you?"

Before I could answer, he said, "You see, my wife of 67 years died on Monday. We received friends at the funeral home on Tuesday. On Wednesday . . ." He paused.

Swallowing hard, he said, "On Wednesday, I buried her.

"On Thursday my out-on-town relatives went back home, and Friday—just yesterday—my children went back to their homes in Greenwood. This morning, I was sitting in my dark living room, crying out loud. I said to God, Who needs an old, wore-out, 86-year-old man? Nobody!

"Then," he said, "You immediately knocked on the door and said, 'Sir, I need you!' When I opened that door, light flooded the room around your head. Are you an angel?"

I assured him I was no angel.

Then I listened as he told all his ideas for a flower ministry, giving his magnolias and also daisies to those who needed encouragement in the neighborhood!

I believe God performed a miracle that day. He knew I could encourage His 86-year-old child, so He moved me out of the church and into the world by sending the storm to destroy my flowers. Then He sent me to the home of His child, in His timing.

God often coincides His will with our needs—performs miracles for His glory![3]

It's a beautiful thing when we can turn our disappointments into a bright light to touch someone else's life. Edna's story reminds us that God can bring beauty even in the midst of disappointments. Life is more meaningful when we touch and bless the lives of others. May the Lord open our eyes to the opportunities to use our disappointments to help lift up another person.

A RAY OF SUNSHINE

Kelsi's smile could melt away anyone's gloomy clouds. Through her many surgeries and treatments, she always seemed to have a grateful spirit and a desire to lift up others. Born with cystic fibrosis as well as other complications, Kelsi was a joyful trooper. Even when she had an oxygen tube in her nose and IV and G-tubes attached to her body, she still managed to smile at visitors and friends. She delivered more joy to others in her short thirteen years on this earth than most people offer to others in an entire lifetime.

Kelsi's family surrounded her with loving care and support, but there was a special and unique bond between Kelsi and her mother, Michelle. Michelle's background is in nursing, so she was able to care for Kelsi's medical needs and tend to her numerous treatments. You can imagine that grief hit Michelle hard when Kelsi went on to her heavenly home.

Eight days after Kelsi's memorial service, an idea came to Michelle. She started a website called Kelsi's Kind Heart (www.kelsiskindheart. com) in order to honor Kelsi's life and carry on her legacy. It is a place of inspiration and hope. Knowing that Kelsi continually showed kindness and thoughtfulness to others, Michelle and her husband founded Kelsi's Kind Heart for the purpose of giving to others who might need a boost and to perform and encourage random acts of kindness. They give away food baskets and gifts to families at Christmas; they give gifts to kids in the hospital. They donate money to the Cystic Fibrosis Foundation. They even started a college scholarship fund in Kelsi's honor for a deserving recipient who is in their county 4-H. Kelsi loved 4-H and even showed her pig one year while carrying her oxygen tank in a backpack!

Michelle began writing thoughts about kindness and poems to

bless others, as it helped her work through some of the grief. Although Michelle still grieves, she has learned to lean on her faith in God and take one day at a time. She has also found strength in the joy of giving to others.

I want to close this chapter not with my words, but with Michelle's. You will be blessed by the insight and wisdom that flows through this precious woman as she reflects on her own daughter's acts of kindness. The following is from Kelsi's Kind Heart website:

When we do good deeds, they usually have a ripple effect. People who have received good deeds or experienced kindness from others realize how good it made them feel or how it helped them. They in turn do a good deed for someone else or sometimes return a favor to the same person. This leads to both parties being blessed, the giver and the receiver.

The Bible says, "There is a time to give and a time to receive." A wise friend reminded us of this once as he was very generously doing a good deed for us. There are times when your deed or kindness can come to the person as they are feeling lost or weary and can change their whole day or attitude. You can lift someone's spirits, more than you would ever realize, with a simple easy gesture of kindness. I encourage you to experience the feeling of giving to others. There are many ways to give, not just monetarily—be creative! The term "Pay it forward" is so important. It doesn't refer to money but to a good deed or kindness.

Here are some examples of things we can do.

1. Hold the door open for the person coming in behind you.
2. Take flowers to an elderly person.
3. Give a positive note or treat to a coworker.
4. When you feel someone has done a great job—tell him or her so.
5. Send a card or note to a person who is in the hospital, ill, or homebound.

6. Send a card or care package of goodies to a child who is in the hospital or sick at home.

7. Write a thank-you note to someone who has made a difference in your life.

8. Forgive someone.

9. Stop for a pedestrian who is waiting to cross the street.

10. Surprise your neighbor with a medium pepperoni pizza—everyone loves pizza. If you order delivery for your family, just order one extra and take it to their house.

11. Let someone with fewer groceries go in front of you.

12. When driving, let someone into your lane if they are trying to get in.

13. Collect items for a food bank or support other causes. Don't always think someone else will do it. Everyone may be thinking the same thing.

14. If you like to bake, take a friend or neighbor some goodies. This is a good way to get your children involved.

15. Smile at someone you come in contact with in your day-to-day life.

16. Send money in a card anonymously to someone who could use a boost; even if it didn't make it to them, you would receive the blessing.

17. The Bible tells us to take care of the widows and orphans. Take food to a widow or widower or just check on them. Donate clothing, food, or toys—especially at Christmas—to a local children's home. This is a special way to get your children involved in helping others. Your children will learn giving and helping from your example.

These are just a few; there are so many others. Always remember that God is who we want to please, impress, and strive to be like—not our peers. Young and old, we all need to remember that.

Are you inspired? I know I was. Please visit the website to read the poems and inspirations written by Michelle and Kelsi's family and friends. These writings will bless you and inspire your kind heart. Certainly we all want to be givers of kindness and bless the people God puts in our lives, just like Kelsi. When we shine God's kindness on others, we ourselves are filled with a thriving joy and peace!

STEPPING FORWARD

 ### POINTS

- Through our pain and experience, we can help others.
- Be open to the opportunities around you and the unique ways God can use you.
- We all have the ability to bless someone else in some way.
- God may use you to touch one person.
- God may use you to help many people.
- Allow his kindness to shine through you to the people you encounter every day.

 ### PASSAGE: ROMANS 12:1–8

Dear brothers and sisters, I plead with you to give your bodies to God because of all he has done for you. Let them be a living and holy sacrifice—the kind he will find acceptable. This is truly the way to worship him. Don't copy the behavior and customs of this world, but let God transform you into a new person by changing the way you think. Then you will learn to know God's will for you, which is good and pleasing and perfect.

Because of the privilege and authority God has given me, I give each of you this warning: Don't think you are better than you really are. Be honest in your evaluation of yourselves, measuring yourselves by the faith God has given us. Just as our bodies have many parts and each part has a special function, so it is with Christ's body. We are many parts of one body, and we all belong to each other.

In his grace, God has given us different gifts for doing certain things well. So if God has given you the ability to prophesy, speak out with as much faith as God has given you. If your gift is serving others, serve them well. If you are a teacher, teach well. If your gift is to encourage others, be encouraging. If it is giving, give generously. If God has given you leadership ability, take the responsibility seriously. And if you have a gift for showing kindness to others, do it gladly.

 PRAYER

God of comfort and strength, I praise you for your goodness and mercy toward me. Thank you for your presence in my life. Thank you for hearing my prayers. Open my eyes to the opportunities around me to bless other people. Change my viewpoint from one of despair to one of care. Show me how to care for the people around me, using the unique gifts you have given me. Thank you, Lord, that you have equipped me to bless others. Give me the courage to step forward. In Jesus' name, amen.

 PLAN

Who can you bless right now? In the space below, write down the name of someone in your life to whom you can reach out and offer help. It may be a smile, a hug, a listening ear, a prayer, a note, a lift to the grocery store, help with the kids, or a meal. Do something, even if it is just a small thing, to lift another person's day. Record what you did on the next lines.

Name:_____

How I reached out to this person: _____

_____

_____

_____

Difficulties are meant to rouse, not discourage.
The human spirit is to grow strong by conflict.

William Ellery Channing

12

Strength of Soul

Discovering Your Capacity to Persevere

On the day I called, you answered me;
my strength of soul you increased.

Psalm 138:3 ESV

T HE BILLBOARD READS, Me Quit? Never. The next line says, Rising above. Pass it on. Beside the text is the picture of a young blond teenager holding a surfboard with her right hand, while her left arm is completely gone. Perhaps you are familiar with the story of Bethany Hamilton, a thirteen-year-old accomplished surfer who survived a severe shark attack off the coast of Kauai, Hawaii, in October 2003.

When Bethany was a young girl, her parents began teaching her how to surf; they also taught her about a relationship with Jesus Christ. Bethany says it was her faith in Christ and his peace that got her through this challenging experience.

Bethany's positive attitude and determination are evident to all who know her. Less than a month after the attack and losing her arm, she went back in the water again. She was determined to reach her goal of being a world champion surfer. As she entered the competitions, she refused special treatment because she wanted to compete on the same level as the other participants. In 2005, she won first place in the NSSA National Championship and now has a long list of accomplishments, awards, and honors. She has been interviewed by national and foreign media and has gone on to write several books and devotionals, including a book about her own story called *Soul Surfer*. Bethany's story is also being made into a feature film.

She says, "My mom and I were praying, before the shark attack, that God would use me." And he has! Her testimony is powerful, and her perseverance offers a picture of hope and resilience to people around the world. Bethany says, "Courage doesn't mean you don't get afraid, courage means you don't let fear stop you."[1] Bethany continues to surf competitively as well as reach out to others with her inspiring message of helping people overcome adversity no matter how great. She is chairperson of the Beating the Odds Foundation and a spokesperson for World Vision. You can read more about her on her website (Bethanyhamilton.com), which states that Bethany's "story is continually growing as she strives to be the best at whatever God calls her to do."[2]

Bethany's determination to do much more than simply survive increases my faith in a God who can give each of us the courage we need to move forward and past our pain. Our determination to persevere is born out of our belief that God is not finished with us yet. He is continuing to unfold a plan that goes beyond our limitations. Bethany didn't call it quits when she lost her arm. Instead, she began to dream of what it would be like to be a one-armed surfer. Bethany had physical strength, but more important, she had strength of soul—a strength only God can give.

> *Our determination to persevere is born out of our belief that God is not finished with us yet.*

Our Souls' Strength

Are you weary? Have you been wounded? Do you feel as though you lack the courage to continue? Are you merely surviving a dismal life? Have you reached a point of defeat? There is a strength that defies human understanding. A hope and determination that can only be supernatural. It is the strength God gives our souls, to help us make it through one more day. We may become discouraged if we focus on three days from now, or three weeks from now, or even how we will do Christmas ever again. We must trust him for today's strength.

Perhaps you are aware of the unique ability of the eagle. These fine birds have a God-given sense about when a storm is approaching. Instead of avoiding the storm, they fly to a higher spot. When the wind comes, they set their wings to pick it up, and that wind allows them to rise above the storm. They actually use the wind from the storm to lift them higher.

> *They actually use the wind from the storm to lift them higher.*

Bethany Hamilton is a beautiful example of allowing an injury to lift one higher and open doors to proclaim God's love and goodness. My friend, you may not yet see how your storm can lift you up, but as you turn to the Lord for strength, he will give you the lift you need to rise above the storm. We can let the storms of life weigh us down, or we can allow God to lift us up to a new level of strength, hope, and faith.

I'm reminded of God's encouragement to the Israelites found in Isaiah:

Do you not know?
Have you not heard?
The Lord is the everlasting God,
the Creator of the ends of the earth.
He will not grow tired or weary,
and his understanding no one can fathom.
He gives strength to the weary
and increases the power of the weak.

Even youths grow tired and weary,
>   and young men stumble and fall;
but those who hope in the LORD
>   will renew their strength.
They will soar on wings like eagles;
>   they will run and not grow weary,
>   they will walk and not be faint.[3]

Strength of soul is a God thing, not a me thing or a you thing. It's that determination to get back on the surfboard

Strength of soul is a God thing, not a me thing or a you thing.

or return to the workplace or simply to enter life again. God has enriched each of our lives with meaning and purpose. He has a plan for our next step, and he will give us the strength to take the next step. As he calls us to do a certain work in this world, he will give us what we need to carry it out.

Waiting on the Lord

Our greatest hardship may come in the form of waiting: waiting for God to change someone's heart, waiting to have a child, waiting for that perfect man to marry, waiting for a spouse to come to the Lord, waiting for acceptance to a school or university. Waiting is never easy, but it is a part of life. In the Bible, we read that innocent Joseph waited in an Egyptian prison for two years before he was released, Hannah waited for a child, Israel waited for a Messiah, and Paul waited in a prison cell. Yet God can use our waiting for a purpose, whether it is to help others or to teach us, strengthen us, or help us grow in our faith.

When life doesn't turn out as we'd planned, we often find ourselves in the waiting room of life. Are you in the waiting room of life? While we're waiting, we often feel so all alone. We feel as if

God doesn't hear our cries for help. It doesn't seem to make sense. I must admit, the only truth that gives my soul strength in the midst of the waiting room is my faith in a God whose timing is better than my own. I see in part, but he sees the whole.

The most loving parents don't give their children everything they ask for (thankfully), and they don't always give them what they want immediately. Our loving heavenly Father bids us to wait sometimes. His loving care

Waiting on the Lord is one of the truest walks of faith, for we wait, not knowing the outcome.

does not spoil us with immediate gratification, but strengthens our faith in him through waiting and watching.

Waiting on the Lord means hoping in him and finding our strength in him. It is one of the truest walks of faith, for we wait, not knowing the outcome. We wait, simply trusting that God loves us and that he works all things together for our good. Allow the following words to draw into your heart and give you strength:

Listen to my voice in the morning, LORD. Each morning I bring my requests to you and *wait* expectantly.[4] —David

Wait patiently for the LORD. Be brave and courageous. Yes, *wait* patiently for the LORD.[5]—David

Be still in the presence of the LORD, and *wait* patiently for him to act. Don't worry about evil people who prosper or fret about their wicked schemes.[6] —David

You are my strength; I *wait* for you to rescue me, for you, O God, are my fortress.[7]—David

Let all that I am *wait* quietly before God, for my hope is in him.[8]—David

I will *wait* for the LORD, who has turned away from the descendants of Jacob. I will put my hope in him.[9] —Isaiah

It is good to *wait* quietly for salvation from the LORD.[10] —Jeremiah

As for me, I look to the LORD for help. I *wait* confidently for God to save me, and my God will certainly hear me.[11]—Micah

God's Word bolsters our strength and helps us endure. As the apostle Paul said, "The Scriptures give us hope and encouragement as we *wait* patiently for God's promises to be fulfilled."[12] Let us lean on the hope we find in God's Word as we wait expectantly for him. If you are in the waiting room of life, I encourage you to spend time daily feeding on God's Word. It is a source of strength we so desperately need to nourish our souls every day.

David found comfort and strength continually in God's Word. He said, "My soul longs for your salvation; I hope in your word. My eyes long for your promise; I ask, 'When will you comfort me?' . . . If your law had not been my delight, I would have perished in my affliction. I will never forget your precepts, for by them you have given me life. I am yours; save me, for I have sought your precepts."[13] We, too, can find strength and comfort as we dwell on God's Word. May we never neglect the wonderful words of encouragement God has given us to strengthen our souls.

The Lord Is Our Keeper

Now and then you meet a thriving woman who has demonstrated strength of soul throughout her life. Helen Hosier is one of those ladies. Although her life is filled with both joy and pain, she has found her strength from the Lord. Her friend Joylynn Reed tells her story:

When you first meet Helen Hosier, you see a well-dressed, beautiful lady. Most would assume that she has spent her days entertaining a bridge group and volunteering on local arts boards. This stereotype could not be further from the truth for this accomplished author. Most noticeable, however, is that after talking with Helen for just a few minutes, you see her love of God radiate even greater than her numerous accomplishments. While many people use their pasts to excuse their present situations, Helen uses hers to demonstrate God's love in her life. She tells her story as an example for others to see how God has given her strength for her soul.

"I was born into a fatherless home; my father died five months before my birth but not before giving me my name. Awaiting my arrival were a ten-year-old brother and a five-year-old sister. We were a mourning family; I think I even cried in the womb."

Helen insists that this wasn't an altogether bad experience because it made her a God-conscious child, and that awareness has never left her. "It propelled me into a lifelong desire to please God and get to know him better. I couldn't have known the word *thrive*, but I can tell you that my mother modeled it. I saw how her unwavering faith in God took her through the hard times. I remember one time saying, 'Oh Mama, I wish you didn't have to work so hard.' She answered, 'I need to keep a roof over our heads, food on the table, and clothes on our backs, but you mustn't worry. God is taking care of us. He sees us through.' She wasn't complaining; she was teaching us that we could trust God. Mother taught us Bible verses that lodged in my heart and have come to my rescue time after time. Some ferocious storms slammed into our lives with frightening ferocity, not all of them caused by the weather! Mother's work ethic and tenacity in the face of hardships provided a powerful demonstration to her children that God was our Stormkeeper."

After high-school graduation, Helen traveled to Washington, DC, to work at the United Nations with the Food and Agriculture Organization. Some months later, when she was offered a position in Southern California, she was awed. She made the cross-country train ride alone. She was thrust into more learning experiences that found her crying out to God for help. What she could not know was that her own ability to thrive, not simply survive, was being formed.

Helen moved her mother from Iowa to California; later she married and began raising a family of four children. While working in Los Angeles, she had discovered Dr. J. Vernon McGee's Church of the Open Door and their Christian bookstore. She spent many noon hours there while a dream began to form in her heart: wouldn't it be wonderful to have such a store! A remarkable series of events saw that dream become a reality when she and her husband opened their first such store in a Los Angeles suburb; still later, after ten years of incredible growth, their second store opened its doors near the well-known Knott's Berry Farm in Buena Park.

But Helen also had a hobby. One night, while reading a little InterVarsity book, *My Heart, Christ's Home*, God put on her heart that if she would give her gift of writing, her hobby, to him, he would bless and use her. She took as her writing verse Colossians 3:23, "And whatever you do, do it heartily, as to the Lord and not to men, knowing that from the Lord you will receive the reward of the inheritance; for you serve the Lord Christ."

She invested seven years writing a weekly column, "Over a Cup of Coffee," for her denomination's magazine, then she spent another three years writing "Hi from Helen" for *Christian Times*, published by Dr. Kenneth Taylor and Tyndale House Publishers, as well as articles for the leading Christian magazines of that era. When the president of the

Fleming H. Revell Company approached her at a Christian Booksellers Convention and suggested she start writing books, she told him, "I don't know how to write books!" That proved to be one of the understatements of the century, for as of this writing, Helen has written more than sixty books. Her first book was published in 1966, followed by, on average, one a year. Excellence in Media in Hollywood, California, recognized Helen's exceptional contributions when they awarded her three silver Angel Awards, and one gold Angel Lifetime Achievement Award in 2001 for her thirty-five years of Christian writing.

Ask Helen what she's doing now, and she will tell you about her four children, ten grandchildren—three in heaven—and four great-grandchildren scattered throughout the country and Canada. And she's still writing! She says, "I need to finish at least some of the manuscripts that are started. God has been so faithful to me, He has been my Keeper, and I'm finishing a book I've titled *The Kept Woman*—God is our Tearkeeper, Lifekeeper, Mercykeeper, Peacekeeper, Waykeeper, Heartkeeper, Deathkeeper, Soulkeeper, and there are more 'Keepers.' As long as God grants me years, I'll continue to write."

Women today are aware that their mothers and older sisters were not readily accepted in professional settings. What they often do not realize, however, are the battles that these trailblazing women fought and the obstacles they overcame. Helen made a living, raised and supported her family, made influential connections, gained respect from leaders, and never wavered from her faith at a time when women were discouraged from doing these things. But this amazing woman did not do it herself; God truly blessed, guided, and prospered Helen. Does she have a favorite Bible verse? "I do especially love this: 'Trust in the Lord with all your heart, and lean not on your own understanding; in all your ways acknowledge Him, and He shall direct your paths.' He is truly our Waykeeper."

Soul's Satisfaction

Waykeeper! I love that term. God guides our paths and leads us along the way as a shepherd leads his precious sheep. We are precious in his sight. He loves us so much he is preparing a place for us in heaven. Our life on earth is short, temporary, and imperfect. Yes, our hearts long for what is beautiful and perfect—the perfect marriage, the perfect vacation, the perfect family—but perfection isn't meant for this world; that's what heaven is for. We wait in anticipation for that day when we will see Jesus face to face.

In his book *Mere Christianity*, C. S. Lewis states, "If I find in myself a desire which no experience in this world can satisfy, the most probable explanation is that I was made for another world."[14] We will never be satisfied on this earth. No circumstance, no place, and no person can completely satisfy the deepest desire in our hearts for the perfect and the beautiful. Our souls long for a better place: a place of satisfaction and completeness. When we live in the presence of God, our souls will be completely satisfied.

> *"If I find in myself a desire which no experience in this world can satisfy, the most probable explanation is that I was made for another world."*
> —C. S. Lewis

We were made for that place. A place where all things will make sense. A place where earthly trials and challenges that loom large for us now will seem small in comparison to the big scheme of eternity. When I think of the apostle Paul, who endured hardships and sufferings in order to fervently proclaim the gospel, I see a man who lived with hope for a better place. Here's what he has to say to us:

What we suffer now is nothing compared to the glory he will reveal to us later. For all creation is waiting eagerly for that future day when God will reveal who his children really are. Against its will, all creation was subjected to God's curse. But with eager hope, the creation looks forward to the day when it will join God's children in glorious freedom from death and decay. For we know that all creation has been groaning as in the pains of childbirth right up to the present time. And we believers also groan, even though we have the Holy Spirit within us as a foretaste of future glory, for we long for our bodies to be released from sin and suffering. We, too, wait with eager hope for the day when God will give us our full rights as his adopted children, including the new bodies he has promised us. We were given this hope when we were saved. (If we already have something, we don't need to hope for it. But if we look forward to something we don't yet have, we must wait patiently and confidently.)[15]

Paul waited with eager hope for his heavenly reward. We experience a great joy when we set our minds on things above in anticipation of our perfect home. British theologian J. C. Ryle said, "I pity the man who never thinks about heaven."[16] It would be a sad existence if this world were all we had to live for. Author Randy Alcorn closes his tremendous book titled *Heaven* (you must read it!) by saying, "We were all made for a person and a place. Jesus is the person. Heaven is the place. If you know Jesus, I'll be with you in that resurrected world. With the Lord we love and with the friends we cherish, we'll embark together on the ultimate adventure, in a spectacular new universe awaiting our exploration and dominion. Jesus will be the center of all things, and joy will be the air we breathe."[17]

Joy will be the very air we breathe! Yes, that's what I look forward to. What about you? How can we passionately live the life we didn't plan? By passionately living for a better place! And so as we walk with the Lord hand in hand, he leads us, strengthens us, and cheers us all along the way. One of my favorite old hymns is "Great Is Thy Faithfulness." Often the words flow through my mind: "Strength for today and bright hope for tomorrow, blessings all mine, with ten thousand beside. Great is Thy faithfulness . . . Morning by morning new mercies I see; All I have needed Thy hand hath provided; Great is Thy faithfulness, Lord, unto me!"[18]

It's obvious that the author of that hymn knew the difference between simply surviving and passionately thriving. May this be the song of our lives, as we walk together with God through the joys and sorrows of life.

STEPPING FORWARD

POINTS

- Courage and the ability to *thrive* come from the Lord.
- Determination and perseverance are qualities of the woman who lives the unplanned life with passion.
- Allow God to lift you above the storms and help you soar.
- Waiting on God is the truest walk of faith.
- The Lord is our keeper through life's journey.
- Our hearts long for a better place, and that place is heaven.

PASSAGE: PSALM 18:1–6, 16–19

I love you, LORD;
    you are my strength.

The LORD is my rock, my fortress, and my savior;
    my God is my rock, in which I find protection.
He is my shield, the power that saves me,
    and my place of safety.
I called on the LORD, who is worthy of praise,
    and he saved me from my enemies.

The ropes of death entangled me;
    floods of destruction swept over me.
The grave wrapped its ropes around me;
    death laid a trap in my path.
But in my distress I cried out to the LORD;
    yes, I prayed to my God for help.
He heard me from his sanctuary;
    my cry to him reached his ears . . .

He reached down from heaven and rescued me;
    he drew me out of deep waters.
He rescued me from my powerful enemies,
    from those who hated me and were too strong for me.
They attacked me at a moment when I was in distress,
    but the LORD supported me.
He led me to a place of safety;
    he rescued me because he delights in me.

 ### PRAYER

Redeeming Lord, you are able to take the storms of life and use them to lift me up to new places. You are the wind that holds me up. You are my keeper, my hope, my strength, and my salvation. My heart waits expectantly to see what you can do, far beyond what I ask or imagine. I believe in you; help my unbelief. Give me strength of soul that the world cannot understand. My eyes are on you. Help me rise above my circumstances, and give me your joy and peace.

 ## PLAN

Write or type and print out the following words from Isaiah 40:28–31 NIV:

Do you not know? Have you not heard? The LORD is the everlasting God, the Creator of the ends of the earth. He will not grow tired or weary, and his understanding no one can fathom. He gives strength to the weary and increases the power of the weak. Even youths grow tired and weary, and young men stumble and fall; but those who hope in the LORD will renew their strength. They will soar on wings like eagles; they will run and not grow weary, they will walk and not be faint.

Underline the phrase that means the most to you right now in your life. Memorize the phrase and bring it to mind whenever you feel weak or weary. Ask God to give you strength of soul, day by day.

Have hope.
Though clouds environs now,
And gladness hides her face in scorn,
Put thou the shadow from thy brow—
No night but hath its morn.

J. C. F. von Schiller

Conclusion

Forward Hope

Recognizing God's Redeeming Work in Your Life

Rejoice in our confident hope.
Be patient in trouble,
and keep on praying.

Romans 12:12

As we have journeyed together through the pages of this book, you have read story upon story of women who found themselves living lives they didn't plan. These courageous women have chosen to do much more than survive; they have learned how to *thrive*. Through the struggles and challenges of life, they have come to a place of hope and renewal. The ability to thrive is not a quality they mustered up on their own; it is a quiet strength God has given them through their personal challenges. As I have collected these stories, I have come to realize that everyone has a story. Certainly some are more dramatic and life-changing than others, but we all have faced disappointments and lost dreams in our lives.

We learn from sharing each other's stories and hearing the voices of hope that ring out from each one. Yet the greatest story ever told is one of redeeming hope. What may have seemed like an unplanned tragedy and disappointment was actually a glorious picture of hope for all mankind. Jesus came to this world in order to bring us hope, hope beyond this world. Without him we are hopelessly lost. You see, the greatest story ever told is that of a loving God, who reached down to sinful men and women and sent his only Son to die on our behalf.

While Jesus was here on earth, he led a perfect life. He preached of love, kindness, forgiveness, and compassion. His fol-

> *The greatest story ever told is that of a loving God, who reached down to sinful men and women and sent his only Son to die on our behalf.*

lowers knew he was the Messiah. In fact, picture the beauty of what we now call Palm Sunday, where Jesus rode into Jerusalem on a donkey and all the crowds hailed him, "Praise God for the Son of David! Blessings on the one who comes in the name of the Lord! Praise God in highest heaven!"[1] The Bible tells us the entire city was in an uproar as he entered. Yet disappointment was soon to follow.

The Messiah, whom the crowds had praised, was tried and sentenced to death by crucifixion a week later. Dejected and discouraged, his disciples dispersed. How could this be God's plan for his gentle and perfect Son to be crucified? It is hard to believe God would plan such a tragedy, but we read in the Old Testament that God planned this long before Jesus was born in a manger. Notice God's specific plan, highlighted in the following passage describing the death of Jesus written by the prophet Isaiah hundreds of years before Jesus walked this earth:

> Who has believed our message?
>> To whom has the LORD revealed his powerful arm?
> My servant grew up in the LORD's presence like a tender
>> green shoot,
>> like a root in dry ground.
> There was nothing beautiful or majestic about his
>> appearance,
>> nothing to attract us to him.

He was despised and rejected—
    a man of sorrows, acquainted with deepest grief.
We turned our backs on him and looked the other way.
    He was despised, and we did not care.

Yet it was our weaknesses he carried;
    it was our sorrows that weighed him down.
And we thought his troubles were a punishment from God,
    a punishment for his own sins!
But he was pierced for our rebellion,
    crushed for our sins.
He was beaten so we could be whole.
    He was whipped so we could be healed.
All of us, like sheep, have strayed away.
    We have left God's paths to follow our own.
Yet the LORD laid on him
    the sins of us all.

He was oppressed and treated harshly,
    yet he never said a word.
He was led like a lamb to the slaughter.
    And as a sheep is silent before the shearers,
    he did not open his mouth.
Unjustly condemned,
    he was led away.
No one cared that he died without descendants,
    that his life was cut short in midstream.
But he was struck down
    for the rebellion of my people.
He had done no wrong
    and had never deceived anyone.
But he was buried like a criminal;
    he was put in a rich man's grave.

But it was the LORD's good plan to crush him
and cause him grief.
Yet when his life is made an offering for sin,
he will have many descendants.
He will enjoy a long life,
and the LORD's good plan will prosper in his hands.
When he sees all that is accomplished by his anguish,
he will be satisfied.
And because of his experience,
my righteous servant will make it possible
for many to be counted righteous,
for he will bear all their sins.
I will give him the honors of a victorious soldier,
because he exposed himself to death.
He was counted among the rebels.
He bore the sins of many and interceded for rebels.[2]

The Lord's Good Plan?

Did you read the words in the passage above, "But it was the LORD's good plan to crush him and cause him grief?" How could it be a good plan for an innocent man to be tortured and die in the most awful of ways, nailed to a cross? It was God's good plan, because it was God's redeeming plan. You see, as a holy and perfect God, he hates sin (not sinners, but sin). God is also a loving God and therefore provided a payment for our sins. Jesus was the sacrifice on our behalf. His death paid for our lives. We are justified through the shedding of his blood.

The Bible says, "For it is by grace you have been saved, through faith—and this not from yourselves, it is the gift of God—not by works, so that no one can boast."[3] I'm so glad God's plan didn't include our trying to work our way to heaven.

We would all fail and miss the mark. Instead, God gave his Son and invites us to trust in him. Jesus gives us a picture of the ultimate tragedy and injustice, which turned out to be the ultimate treasure of God's grace toward mankind. My friend, do you believe?[4]

His story can become your story. God's redeeming work did not stop with the cross. Not only can God redeem your life, but he can redeem your situation. You may be steeped in disbelief. You may have lost hope. Although you cannot see the end of the tunnel, there is hope. Just as the defeated disciples lost their picture of hope on Friday, Sunday was coming. Christ rose from the dead, giving them the ultimate hope of eternal life one day in heaven. You may be asking, why did this have to happen to me or my child or my family? I'm sure the disciples were asking the same thing. Can you trust that God has a greater plan, a bigger and more eternal one?

It's not easy to have that kind of hope, I know. But God is in the hope business. Ask God to renew your hope and give you what you need for today. My prayer for you is the same as Paul's: "I pray that God, the source of hope, will fill you completely with joy and peace because you trust in him. Then you will overflow with confident hope through the power of the Holy Spirit."[5] The power to thrive doesn't come from ourselves, it comes from the God who loves us and redeems the broken pieces of our lives.

> *God is in the hope business. Ask God to renew your hope and give you what you need for today.*

As I write this final paragraph, I want you to know my thoughts and prayers go with you. I may not know you personally, but I do know your pathway has had struggles. I know you need the Lord just as much as I do. We all need him. Not one of us can weather the storms alone, and I want to give you the opportunity to share the story of how you learned to thrive, not simply survive. If you go to PositiveLifePrinciples.com and click on *Thrive, Don't Simply Survive*, you will find your place. I can't guarantee I will post every story that comes my way, but each month I will post at least one. This website will allow you to see that you are not alone and that God brings beauty from ashes.

Leader's Guide
for Study Groups

*T*HRIVE, DON'T SIMPLY SURVIVE: *Passionately Live the Life You Didn't Plan* makes a perfect group study whether you are drawing women together in the neighborhood or at work or at your church. The name itself speaks to every woman's life in some form or fashion. My prayer is that God will use this book to build bonds and open doors of communication between women. The following study, which uses this book, allows women to gently remove the "I've got my life all together" mask and instead be open, honest, and real with one another. Ultimately my desire for this book is to bring every reader into a deeper relationship with Christ.

If you are the leader of the group study, allow me to share a few tips with you as you embark on this journey. Since there are twelve chapters in this book, I recommend you study one chapter per meeting, assigning the women to read the chapter and answer the questions in this section. Your first time together should be an introductory meeting to get to know the ladies in the group and talk about how you plan to do the study. You may want to point out a few features about the book such as the Stepping Forward section at the end of each chapter, which includes the key points, a prayer, a Scripture passage to ponder, and a plan of action. For your first meeting, you may want to highlight a few quotes or tidbits from the introduction of the book to share with the ladies. Also, be sure to visit my website (PositiveLifePrinciples.com) for a free, downloadable flier for the *Thrive, Don't Simply Survive* study.

Each time you meet, I encourage you to open your time together with prayer and then move into the discussion questions in this section. Don't expect every woman to answer every question; just offer the question and allow several ladies to respond. If you notice someone is dominating the conversation, ask a quieter person if she would like to share her thoughts. After you have finished the discussion questions, invite the women to share some of the points they highlighted within the chapter, and see if anyone had a chance to carry out the plan of action at the end of the chapter. You may want to encourage everyone to do the plan as a part of their weekly assignment. Close your time together in prayer, specifically praying for any needs or requests mentioned during your time together.

Precious and faithful leader, I want to personally ask you to seek God's guidance and wisdom as you lead this group. Ask him to give you ears to hear the heartfelt needs of the women in your group. This book will most likely become more than just a group study; it can become a circle of fellowship, support, strength, and encouragement for all who participate. You are God's vessel, and his Holy Spirit is the teacher. May he pour his love through you as you touch the lives of the women in your group. My prayers are with you as well. Please feel free to email me and tell me about your group so I can be praying for you specifically: (karolladd@ PositiveLifePrinciples.com).

DISCUSSION QUESTIONS

Chapter 1: Seven Common Disappointments in a Woman's Life

1. Which of the seven common disappointments can you best relate to in your life right now?

2. How does it comfort you to know you are not alone in your struggles?

3. What do you find encouraging or helpful about Jeremiah's words presented in this chapter?

4. How did the poem "The Weaver" specifically speak to you? (See page 17.)

5. As you read Psalm 139:7–18, what words or phrases reassure you that God is with you and has a plan for your life?

Chapter 2: Time to Let Go

1. What words would you use to describe the emotions you have felt through disappointing circumstances in your life? (anger, hurt, loneliness, pain, etc).

2. In what ways have you seen God's care for you in the midst of difficult times? What do you most often thank God for?

3. Are there any past situations you are currently replaying in your head? What are some good, godly, and forgiving thoughts you can play instead?

4. What old dreams do you need to let go of as you begin to step forward into the new plan God has for you?

5. In the passage from Habakkuk (3:17–19), how is it possible for the prophet to say he will be "joyful in . . . God" although it seems like everything is going wrong in his life?

Chapter 3: Worry and What-Ifs

1. What distinct differences do you see between being a worrier and being a responsible person?

2. We have all wasted time needlessly worrying or fretting about something. Describe one of those times in your life.

3. What spoke to you personally in the story about:

    - Moses' talk with God—

    - Martha's feeling overwhelmed—

    - The disciples' fear of sinking—

4. How does our pride get in the way of trusting God with our worries?

5. In what ways do you see God's sovereignty revealed through the words in Psalm 46:1–11?

Chapter 4: How Can I Trust a God Who Allows Pain and Suffering?

1. Has there been a time in your life when you questioned God or were angry at him over a particularly difficult time in your life? How did you work through your feelings?

2. What benefit or blessing have you experienced as a result of a disappointment or challenge you went through in your life?

3. How did Dr. Paul Lanier's view of divine grace speak to you personally?

4. In what ways is it possible to feel God's love even in the midst of trials?

5. As you read Psalm 103:1–13, how do you see yourself in relationship to God?

Chapter 5: The Beauty of Plan B

1. How is your current life different than what you planned or dreamed of as a young woman?

2. Why do you think some people hesitate to approach God with their disappointments or to seek his help discovering possibilities?

3. Tell about a time in your life when you had to trust God in faith even though you couldn't see the end result?

4. Is there an area of your life that needs to change?

5. Prayerfully consider this question: what steps do you believe the Lord is leading you to take toward a new direction?

6. Name several ways God is described in Psalm 62. How is this description meaningful to you?

Chapter 6: The Bitterness Battle

1. Describe a time in your life when you had to choose whether to be bitter or better.

2. What good can result from your decision to love and forgive others?

3. What harm is done when we are consumed with bitterness and self-pity?

4. Letting go of bitterness involves forgiveness, acceptance,

and changing the way we act toward our enemies. Is there a situation in your life right now in which you need to practice these principles?

5. How does the Colossians 3 passage challenge you in your life right now?

Chapter 7: Big-Picture Thinking

1. Why does our perspective make a difference in how we deal with our circumstances?

2. What seems to cloud your heavenly view and distract you from living with an eternal perspective?

3. How has reading and meditating on God's Word helped you gain a better perspective on life?

4. Like the artist in India, is there some trash (frustrations or disappointments) that you need to see as potential treasures (life lessons, maturity, and growth opportunities) in your life right now?

5. As you read Psalm 119:25–40, underline some of the personal benefits of dwelling on God's Word.

Chapter 8: You Are What You Say

1. If your family and friends were to describe you based on the things you say, how would they identify you?

2. In what ways do you use your words for good and to bless others?

3. In the section called "Practically Speaking," which tips do you

want to apply to your life to help you speak in a more positive tone?

4. As followers of Christ, what impact do you think we could have on our communities if we spoke words of faith and hope as opposed to grumbling and complaining?

5. Underline every phrase in Psalm 71:7–21 that talks about using our words for God's glory. How does this passage inspire you to use your words for good?

Chapter 9: Your Confident Stride

1. How has the school of hard knocks (learning through challenges) shaped your life?

2. Why is the first step forward always the most difficult and significant one? Share one of your first steps and your experiences in taking it.

3. What distinguishes self-confidence from God-confidence? Which type of confidence do you tend to lean on in your own struggles?

4. Which of the tips for spiritually good posture do you find most helpful and applicable to your situation or struggle?

5. Describe the confidence and strength you receive from the words in Psalm 86:1–13.

Chapter 10: Healthy Connections

1. Who has God placed in your life to help you through difficult times?

2.   Have you made new friends as you walked through a disappointment or life challenge? How did God use them to bless you and help you?

3.   Why do we tend to push people away sometimes when we are in the midst of hurt and struggle?

4.   Is there a relationship you need to work on in your life right now?

5.   How does Romans 12:9–16 speak to our need for one another?

Chapter 11: Life Is Not a Spectator Sport

1.   What opportunities are there for you to care for others and show compassion to people in your community?

2.   Why is it that reaching out to others tends to bring healing to our own lives?

3.   If you don't feel like a compassionate person or don't know where to begin, to whom can you go for help?

4.   Which of the random acts of kindness listed by Michelle (Kelsi's mom) do you think you can implement this week? (See pages 187 to 188.)

5.   As you read Romans 12:1–8, what gifts do you recognize God has given you to bless other people?

Chapter 12: Strength of Soul

1.   How would you describe "strength of soul" in a woman's life?

2. In what ways were you personally inspired by the stories of Bethany and Helen?

3. Describe a time when you had to wait on the Lord.

4. When you think about heaven, what do you most look forward to?

5. Which words give strength to your soul from Psalm 18:1–6, 16–19?

Dear friends, I hope this has been a pleasant and healing journey for you as you have walked through the pages of this book with your friends. I encourage you to keep walking, as you stroll hand in hand with the Lord through your future joys and struggles. He will never leave you. He has created you for a passionate life that looks beyond mere survival to vibrant thriving. May you feel the joy of his presence and the strength of his loving arms as you take one step at a time down the path he has set before you.

You have to accept whatever comes
and the only important thing is that you meet it with
the best you have to give.
Eleanor Roosevelt

Notes

Introduction

1. See Psalm 103:4–5 NIV.

Chapter 1: Seven Common Disappointments in a Woman's Life

1. See 1 Peter 5:7.

2. See, for example, Genesis 26:24; Isaiah 43:5; Jeremiah 1:8.

3. Psalm 139:7.

4. Matthew 11:28.

5. See Deuteronomy 4:29; Jeremiah 29:13.

6. Exodus 34:6 NIV.

7. See Genesis 4:1–16.

8. Matthew 11:3.

9. Psalm 34:18 NIV.

10. Psalm 43:5 NIV.

11. Lamentations 3:19–26.

12. Psalm 34:19.

13. Nehemiah 8:10.

14. John 15:10–11.

15. Corrie ten Boom, *Messages of God's Abundance* (Grand Rapids, Mich.: Zondervan, 2002), 62–63.

Chapter 2: Time to Let Go

1. Steve Blow, "Making the Best of a Worst Situation," *Dallas Morning News,* January 13, 2008, B1–B2.

2. Psalm 147:3 NIV.

3. John Cook, comp., *The Book of Positive Quotations* (Minneapolis, Minn.: Fairview, 1993), 541.

4. Ruth 1:20–21.

5. Ecclesiastes 3:1, 4.

6. Angela Beasley Freeman, comp., *100 Years of Women's Wisdom* (Nashville, Tenn.: Walnut Grove, 1999), 116.

7. Philippians 4:19.

8. Philippians 3:13–14.

9. Luke 17:32.

10. Luke 23:43.

11. Roy B. Zuck, comp., *The Speaker's Quote Book* (Grand Rapids, Mich.: Kregel, 1997), 180.

Chapter 3: Worry and What-Ifs

1. Visit Jane's website at www.JaneJarrell.net for more info about her and her books.

2. Matthew 6:31–34.

3. Exodus 3:11–12.

4. Exodus 4:1.

5. Exodus 4:10.

6. Exodus 4:11–12.

7. See Habakkuk 3:19.

8. Exodus 4:13.

9. Psalm 37:3–7.

10. See Luke 9:10–17.

11. Luke 10:40.

12. Luke 10:41–42.

13. See Isaiah 63:1.

14. See Mark 4:35–41.

15. 2 Peter 1:3–4.

16. 1 Peter 5:7.

17. Philippians 4:6–8.

Chapter 4: How Can I Trust a God Who Allows Pain and Suffering?

1. Ravi Zacharias and Norman Geisler, *Who Made God? and Answers to Over 100 Other Tough Questions of Faith* (Grand Rapids, Mich.: Zondervan, 2003), 46.

2. Job 38:4.

3. Job 42:2–3, 5.

4. Judge and Amy Reinhold, comp., *Be Still* (West Monroe, La.: Howard, 2007), 72.

5. John Blanchard, ed., *More Gathered Gold* (Hertfordshire, England: Evangelical Press, 1986), 28.

6. 2 Corinthians 4:7–12, 16–17 NIV.

7. James 1:2–4.

8. 2 Corinthians 1:3–6.

9. Psalm 138:6–8.

10. Psalm 25:8–9.

11. Hebrews 12:7–11 NIV.

12. 1 Peter 4:12–13.

13. Paul Lanier, MD, with Dave Turtletaub, *A Change in the Flight Plan* (Dallas, Tex.: Flight Plan Resources, 2006).

14. Charles Haden Spurgeon, *Morning and Evening Daily Readings* (Ross-shire, Scotland: Christian Focus Publications, 1994), February 18.

15. Romans 5:1–5.

16. See Exodus 34:6; Nehemiah 9:17; Psalm 86:15 NIV.

Chapter 5: The Beauty of Plan B

1. Hebrews 4:15–16 NIV.

2. Marcus Dods, *The Prayer That Teaches Us to Pray* (Oxford, England: Oxford University Press, 1885), 18.

3. Mark 9:22–24.

4. Hebrews 11:1 NIV.

5. Psalm 121:2–3, 5 ESV.

6. Hebrews 11:6.

7. John Blanchard, ed., *More Gathered Gold: A Treasury of Quotations for Christians* (Hertfordshire, England: Evangelical Press, 1986), 112.

8. Psalm 51:7–12.

9. Proverbs 27:17.

10. See Proverbs 16:1.

11. Psalm 16:5 NIV.

12. Psalm 33:11.

13. Psalm 138:8.

14. I Chronicles 29:11–13.

15. Daniel 4:34–35.

16. For more about Cyndee's ministry, go to www .specialneedswhatnow.com.

Chapter 6: The Bitterness Battle

1. Ephesians 4:26–27.

2. Ephesians 4:31–32.

3. Luke 23:34.

4. Luke 6:27–38 NIV.

5. See Psalm 103:6.

6. Colossians 3:13 NIV.

Chapter 7: Big-Picture Thinking

1. http://www.e-tutor.com/eNews/issue0705/.

2. http://wendikelly.wordpress.com/2008/04/01/planning-for-the-fog/.

3. Hebrews 12:1–3.

4. See, for example, Deuteronomy 9:6.

5. Joshua 1:8–9 NIV.

6. Joyce Huggett source: *Spiritual Classics*, compiled by Richard Foster and Emile Griffin (New York, N.Y.: HarperCollins, 2000), p. 10, 11.

7. Matthew 19:26 NIV.

8. Philippians 1:21 NIV.

9. Richard Foster, quoted in *Be Still*, compiled by Amy and Judge Reinhold (West Monroe, La.: Howard, 2007), 16.

10. Judge and Amy Reinhold, comp., *Be Still* (West Monroe, La.: Howard, 2007), 19.

11. *Valyermo Benedictine* 1, no.1 (1990), available at www.valyermo.com/ld-art.html. You can find out more about the Benedictine monks of Saint Andrews Abbey by visiting their website at www.Valyermo.com.

12. http://clt.astate.edu/elind/nc_chandig.htm/ and http://mosaicartsource.wordpress.com/2008/03/08/creative-genius-or-just-your-typical-mosaic-artist-with-a-touch-of-ocd-nek-chand-chandigarh-india/

13. 2 Kings 6:14–17.

14. You can learn more about Autumn Ater's ministry by going to www.aholeinmyheart.com.

Chapter 8: You Are What You Say

1. Matthew 12:33–35.

2. Psalm 141:3 NIV.

3. Romans 10:15, Isaiah 52:7 NIV.

4. Romans 10:13.

5. Proverbs 18:4.

6. Proverbs 18:7.

7. Psalm 34:1.

8. Elisabeth Elliot, *A Path through Suffering* (Ann Arbor, Mich.: Servant, 1990), 59–60.

9. Romans 8:28.

10. See Jeremiah 42:11.

11. Psalm 9:1–2.

12. 2 Timothy 3:16.

13. Psalm 119:11.

14. Philippians 2:14–15.

15. Ecclesiastes 4:9–10.

16. Psalm 136:1.

17. 1 Thessalonians 5:16–18.

Chapter 9: Your Confident Stride

1. Anne Beiler, *Twist of Faith* (Nashville, Tenn.: Thomas Nelson, 2008), cover.

2. Psalm 37:23–24.

3. Psalm 71:5 NIV.

4. Proverbs 3:25–27 NIV.

5. Proverbs 14:26–27 ESV.

6. Jeremiah 17:7.

7. 2 Corinthians 3:4–5 NIV.

8. John Cook, comp., *The Book of Positive Quotations* (Minneapolis, Minn.: Fairview, 1993), 114.

9. Psalm 27:13–14.

10. Proverbs 3:3–4 NKJV.

11. Matthew 7:24–27.

12. 2 Corinthians 5:6–10.

13. Peggy Anderson, comp., *Great Quotes from Great Women* (Lombard, Ill.: Celebrating Excellence, 1992), 99.

14. See Psalm 46:1 NKJV.

Chapter 10: Healthy Connections

1. Proverbs 17:17 MSG.

2. Proverbs 18:24.

3. Ephesians 3:20 NIV.

Chapter 11: Life Is Not a Spectator Sport

1. Luke 10:30–35.

2. Exodus 34:6 NIV.

3. Taken from *A Month of Miracles* by coauthor Edna Ellison. Used by permission © 2008 New Hope Publishers, Birmingham, Ala. Available from 1-800-968-7301 or www. newhopepubl.com.

Chapter 12: Strength of Soul

1. *Guideposts for Teens,* June/July 2004.

2. BethanyHamilton.com.

3. Isaiah 40:28–31 NIV.

4. Psalm 5:3.

5. Psalm 27:14.

6. Psalm 37:7.

7. Psalm 59:9.

8. Psalm 62:5.

9. Isaiah 8:17.

10. Lamentations 3:26.

11. Micah 7:7.

12. Romans 15:4.

13. Psalms 119:81–82, 92–94 ESV.

14. C. S. Lewis, *Mere Christianity* (New York, N.Y.: Macmillan, 1952), 120.

15. Romans 8:18–25.

16. J. C. Ryle, *Heaven* (Ross-shire, Scotland: Christian Focus Pub-lications, 2000), 19.

17. Randy Alcorn, *Heaven* (Wheaton, Ill.: Tyndale, 2004), 457.

18. "Great Is Thy Faithfulness," words by Thomas O. Chisholm, *The Baptist Hymnal* (Nashville, Tenn.: Convention Press, 1991), 54.

Conclusion: Forward Hope

1. Matthew 21:9.

2. Isaiah 53.

3. Ephesians 2:8–9 NIV.

4. If you want to talk with someone about faith in Christ, you can call 866-NEED-HIM and talk to someone right now.

5. Romans 15:13.

About the Author

KAROL LADD is making a positive impact in the lives of women around the world. As the bestselling author of over twenty books, including *The Power of a Positive Woman* and *The Power of a Positive Mom*, she shares a message of inspiration, hope, and biblical truth. A graduate of Baylor University, Karol is a gifted and creative communicator offering positive principles for life to businesses, churches, and organizations. She serves on the board of directors for several national ministries and leads a monthly Bible study called "The Positive Woman Connection," which draws women of all denominations to study God's Word together. Karol lives in Texas with her husband, Curt, and daughters, Grace and Joy. Visit her website at www.PositiveLifePrinciples.com.